THE
FIELD&
STREAM
Turkey Hunting
Handbook

The *Field & Stream* Fishing and Hunting Library

HUNTING

The Field & Stream *Bowhunting Handbook* by Bob Robb

The Field & Stream *Deer Hunting Handbook* by Jerome B. Robinson

The Field & Stream *Firearms Safety Handbook* by Doug Painter

The Field & Stream *Shooting Sports Handbook* by Thomas McIntyre

The Field & Stream *Turkey Hunting Handbook* by Philip Bourjaily

The Field & Stream *Upland Bird Hunting Handbook* by Bill Tarrant

FISHING

The Field & Stream *Baits and Rigs Handbook* by C. Boyd Pfeiffer

The Field & Stream *Bass Fishing Handbook* by Mark Sosin and Bill Dance

The Field & Stream *Fish Finding Handbook* by Leonard M. Wright, Jr.

The Field & Stream *Fishing Knots Handbook* by Peter Owen

The Field & Stream *Fly Fishing Handbook* by Leonard M. Wright, Jr.

The Field & Stream *Tackle Care and Repair Handbook* by C. Boyd Pfeiffer

THE
FIELD&
STREAM
Turkey Hunting
Handbook

Philip Bourjaily

THE LYONS PRESS

For
John Bourjaily

Photographs by Philip Bourjaily unless otherwise noted.

10 9 8 7 6 5 4 3 2 1

Printed in the United States of America

Library of Congress Cataloging-in-Publication Data

Bourjaily, Philip.
    The Field & stream turkey hunting handbook / Philip Bourjaily
        p.   cm. — (Field & stream fishing and hunting library)
    Includes index.
    ISBN 1-55821-913-7
    1. Turkey hunting.   I. Title.   II. Title: Field and stream turkey hunting handbook.   III. Series.
    SK325.T8B67   1999
    799.2'4645—dc21   99-10279
                                                      CIP

Contents

Acknowledgments

Any acknowledgments must begin and end with thanks to my wife Pamela, a full-time mom who still finds time to edit my copy, keep my records, and take care of my idiot of an English setter while I'm off chasing turkeys.

I want to thank my editor at The Lyons Press, Jay Cassell, with whom it was a pleasure to work once again. Thanks, too, to the editors at *Field & Stream:* Duncan Barnes, Slaton White, David Petzal, Mike Toth, Jean McKenna, Melissa Van Loan, and Anthony Licata.

Camille Roberge-Meyers at the National Wild Turkey Federation and Andrea Flanigan at Outlaw Decoys both scrambled to meet last-minute requests for photos and information.

I've been lucky enough to hunt and talk turkey with some of the very best hunters in the country; you'll see them quoted throughout this book. All of them have been more than patient with my questions.

Finally, thanks to the turkeys themselves, who hung tough for three hundred years while our ancestors did their level best to kill them all. Welcome back. The woods weren't the same without you.

Acknowledgments

Any acknowledgments must begin and end with thanks to my wife Pamela, a full-time mom who still finds time to edit my copy, keep my records, and take care of my idiot of an English setter while I'm off chasing turkeys.

I want to thank my editor at The Lyons Press, Jay Cassell, with whom it was a pleasure to work once again. Thanks, too, to the editors at *Field & Stream:* Duncan Barnes, Slaton White, David Petzal, Mike Toth, Jean McKenna, Melissa Van Loan, and Anthony Licata.

Camille Roberge-Meyers at the National Wild Turkey Federation and Andrea Flanigan at Outlaw Decoys both scrambled to meet last-minute requests for photos and information.

I've been lucky enough to hunt and talk turkey with some of the very best hunters in the country; you'll see them quoted throughout this book. All of them have been more than patient with my questions.

Finally, thanks to the turkeys themselves, who hung tough for three hundred years while our ancestors did their level best to kill them all. Welcome back. The woods weren't the same without you.

THE
FIELD&
STREAM
Turkey Hunting
Handbook

Introduction

THE FIRST TURKEY I ever called to hopped off a branch at sunrise and walked right to me. Forty yards from the spot where I sat in the Iowa River–bottom mud, the gobbler stepped conveniently behind a large oak, waiting while I remembered to shoulder my bird gun and slip off the safety.

The gun was up and ready when the turkey stepped out the other side. As the tom passed the brush pile I'd picked as my 35-yard marker, I put the bead on his neck and pulled the trigger.

After the gun boomed and the turkey stopped kicking, and my heart slowed down, I lifted the bird by its red, scaled legs. Awkwardly I hoisted the 21-pound gobbler, the bird far bigger than I had ever imagined a wild turkey would be. Mud covered the bright red head. Not knowing what else to do, I carried it over to a small slough and washed it off. Seen up close, the turkey's feathers shimmered with a delicate iridescence. It was quite different from the few turkeys I'd seen before this one, which had always looked almost solidly black as they ran or flew away from me in the timber.

I stood blinking in the bright dawn of an April morning. Around me, birds sang, wood ducks flew through the timber, and the buds of early spring were just beginning to tint the woods a faint green. One thought registered very clearly in my sleep-starved mind: Spring would never be the same again. Nor has it been. It's not the fishing tackle catalogs that see me through the dead months of late winter anymore, but rather a growing assortment of wood, glass, slate, and rubber callers that, even when used the right way, emit the not-so-soothing tone of fingernails on a blackboard. Come spring, the alarm rings at 3:30 A.M. all too often, yet my own biological clock never resets to the notion of getting up at the tail end of the middle of the night. April was once just another month to mark off the calender during the interminable wait between hunting seasons. Now it *is* hunting season. October was already a time when too many good

1

things happened at once. Now there's one more reason—fall turkey hunting—to wish the month had 40 or 50 days.

Welcome to turkey hunting.

A dozen years ago, when I shot that first gobbler, turkeys and successful turkey hunters were rare in my part of the country. At the local sporting goods store, they took my picture and pinned it to the bulletin board. I'm beaming but haggard, dressed in muddy duck-hunting clothes, standing up and holding the bird upside down by the feet (who knew how to hold a turkey?). What call did I use? they asked me. "The red one," I said blankly. There were perhaps three or four other pictures posted that spring.

Go to that same store today in May and the board is covered with row upon row of snapshots, the successful hunters kneeling and beaming behind spread turkey fans. They're dressed for the most part in bark-patterned clothes designed for turkey hunting. They hold short-barreled, sling-swiveled, sometimes scope-sighted shotguns dipped in camo to match their outfits. Their turkey calls have names like "Triple Raspy Split 3.5."

Turkey-hunting gear may have changed a great deal in 12 short years, but the wide smile and bleary eyes of the successful turkey hunter remain the same, always.

In this book, I'll help you as best I can to outfit yourself for turkey hunting in the chapters on calls, guns and gear. Throughout the remainder, I'll share my experiences and those of several experts to help you in scouting, hunting, calling, and, with luck, shooting your spring gobbler. As your turkey-hunting horizons expand, you might find that the chapters on western birds, boating for turkeys, and fall hunting stir your interest. I hope the advice in this book gets you dressed up for turkey hunting and safely pointed in the right direction. The smile and the bleary eyes you'll have to earn on your own.

About Turkeys

I F YOU PICKED this book up, you're a turkey hunter or you're thinking of becoming one. You might live anywhere from Maine to Hawaii; yet chances are you can hear turkeys gobble a short drive from your home.

Five subspecies of our largest upland gamebird live in every state but Alaska, thriving in habitats as diverse as Florida's near-tropical swamps to Minnesota's farms. Today, there are around 4 million wild turkeys in America. Only 70 years ago turkeys roosted on the brink of extinction. The comeback of the wild turkey stands as a tribute to the dedication of sportspeople and wildlife professionals and as a testament to the adaptability of this fascinating bird.

SUBSPECIES

The turkey, of course, is not from Turkey at all but is indigenous to North America. Europeans looked at the big, bareheaded birds and assumed they were giant guineafowl, which in those days were called "turkey cocks." The name stuck.

Four main subspecies of wild turkeys inhabit the United States, although there's considerable overlap and interbreeding among them in some places. When turkey hunters speak of the "Grand Slam" they're talking about bagging an eastern wild turkey, a Rio Grande turkey, a Merriam's turkey, and an Osceola, or Florida, turkey. A fifth subspecies, the Gould's turkey, lives primarily in Mexico, although a few birds range north of the border into New Mexico and Arizona. Here's a short guide to the four subspecies of the Grand Slam:

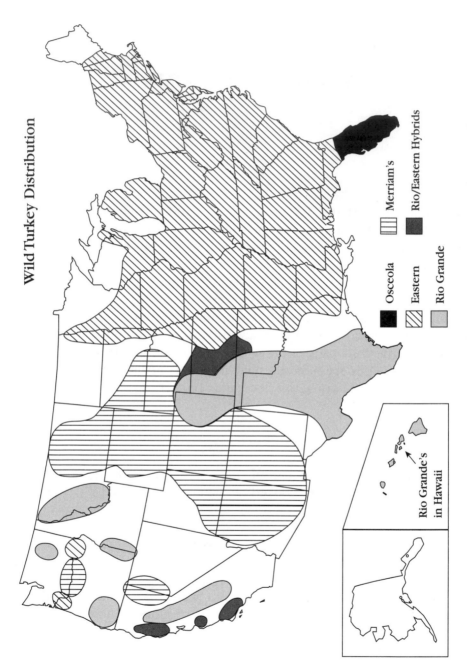

Wild Turkey Distribution

Osceola

Eastern

Rio Grande

Merriam's

Rio/Eastern Hybrids

Rio Grande's in Hawaii

The five subspecies of wild turkeys and their hybrids may be found in every state but Alaska.

The Eastern Wild Turkey

This subspecies is the most widespread and abundant, found in 38 states and Ontario. Three million easterns range from the East Coast to Texas, Missouri, parts of Kansas, Oklahoma and Nebraska, Iowa and Minnesota. Transplanted easterns thrive outside their original range—in Oregon, Washington, and California as well. Their scientific name, *Meleagris gallopavo silvestris,* means "forest turkey," and the eastern is indeed a bird of hardwood timbers, although it also adapts readily to swamps and farm country. The biggest of the four main subspecies, easterns can weigh as much as 30 pounds in the northern part of their range, although 20-plus pounds is more common for gobblers, 8 to 12 pounds for hens. Eastern wild hens and gobblers both may be identified by the chocolate-colored tips of their tailfeathers.

Rio Grande Turkey

Rio Grande turkeys inhabit the wide-open arid spaces of Texas, Oklahoma, and Kansas. Second only to the eastern in population, Rios number over 600,000 birds and have been transplanted far beyond their home range to the Pacific Northwest. The tips of a Rio's tailfeathers are tan, darker than a Merriam's tail but lighter than an eastern's, hence the scientific name—*Meleagris gallopavo intermedia*—because Rios are halfway in between eastern and western turkeys in appearance. In Kansas especially, where easterns and Rios' ranges overlap, there is a large population of Rio/eastern hybrids. Gobblers weigh 20 pounds, hens 8 to 12 pounds.

The Merriam's Turkey

Named for C. Hart Merriam, the first chief of the U.S. Biological Survey, *Meleagris gallopavo merriami* inhabit the ponderosa pines of the mountain west. Like elk and mule deer, Merriam's turkeys will migrate from high country to low with the onset of winter, returning

Writer L. P. Brezny and calling champion Eddie Salter teamed up on this Osceola gobbler. Note the dark-barred primary feathers. *Photo by Julia C. McClellan.*

to higher elevations in the spring. Nearly as big as eastern wild turkeys, Merriam's are easily distinguished from *silvestris* by their white-edged fans and rump feathers. Historically found in Colorado, New Mexico, and Arizona, the Merriam's has adapted to the northern mountain states as well as the prairies of South Dakota and Nebraska and parts of the Pacific northwest. In all, the Merriam's population totals around 200,000.

The Osceola or Florida Turkey

Meleagris gallopavo Osceola, named for the famous Seminole chief, may be found only in the pine woods and cypress swamps of the Florida peninsula. With a population of around 80,000, the Osceola is the least numerous of the four main subspecies. Smaller but similar in appearance to easterns, Osceolas can best be identified by

Eastern wild turkeys can live in a variety of habitats, from midwestern farmland to this South Carolina swamp.

their darker-barred primary feathers. Gobblers weigh less than 20 pounds.

HABITAT REQUIREMENTS

All turkeys must roost off the ground out of reach of nocturnal predators. Most eastern turkeys roost in hardwoods; Merriam's use ponderosa pines, and Osceolas often choose cypress trees. Rio Grande turkeys may prefer a tall cottonwood, but in the absence of suitable trees Rios will roost on power lines and windmill towers.

Newly hatched turkeys need the protein they get from a diet of insects. At one month of age they switch over to plant matter. For the rest of their lives, they will feed primarily on nuts, seeds, leaves, and berries. Adult turkeys sometimes eat ants, bees, grasshoppers, caterpillars, crickets, even fish and an occasional salamander. Birds in the northern states will supplement their diet with corn as a source of high energy during winter.

Turkeys usually feed twice a day, although gobblers hardly eat at all during the spring breeding season. Instead, they rely on the fat stored over the winter in their "breast sponge" to see them through the courtship battles of spring.

Turkeys are gregarious flocking birds with a well-developed social pecking order. They're vocal and for the most part seek out other turkeys. Whereas eastern and Osceola turkeys occupy a fairly small home range, Rios and Merriams may travel miles in a day in search of food and water.

In the spring, the winter flocks break up and gobblers fight to establish dominance. Displaying and gobbling to attract hens, the dominant or "boss" gobbler does most of the breeding. Hens nest by making a depression in the ground, then lay an egg a day until they have a clutch of around 12. After a 28-day incubation period, the poults hatch and quickly grow feathers. At 10 to 12 days of age, young turkeys can fly. By the next spring, the birds of the year are sexually mature. One-year-old males, known as jakes, usually aren't as big as full-grown toms. Jakes sport short, ½-inch to 2½-inch beards, and their central tail feathers are longer than the rest. Turkeys reach full adult size in two years. One way to age a tom is by the spurs. Jakes have no more than a nub on the back of their legs, whereas two-year-old birds' spurs measure up to an inch. Three-year and older toms grow sharp "hooks" over an inch long. Although turkeys have been known to live up to 10 years in captivity, they rarely last longer than 5 years in the wild.

Bobcats, coyotes, foxes, great horned owls, and golden eagles all prevent turkeys from attaining ripe old age. An adult wild turkey, however, is no easy prey even for the fiercest predator. Turkeys can run 12 m.p.h. and fly at 35 m.p.h. for short distances, and if need be they can fight back with their wings and spurs.

Turkeys have remarkably sharp eyesight, with excellent daylight vision and keen color perception. A turkey's peripheral vision extends an impressive 300 degrees. He can periscope his long neck until his eyes are nearly 4 feet off the ground, which enables him to spot danger even when facing the other direction. Turkeys also rely on sharp hearing to detect predators. The turkey's sense of smell,

L-R: *1 YR., 2 YRS., 3+ YRS.*

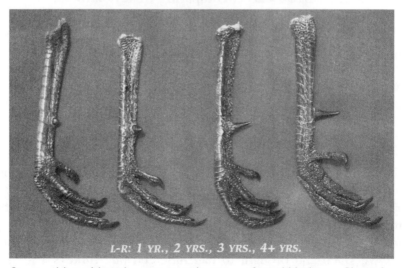

L-R: *1 YR., 2 YRS., 3 YRS., 4+ YRS.*

Spur and beard length are two indications of a gobbler's age. *Photos by Gene Smith. Courtesy of NWTF.*

however, is not well developed. Hunters like to say if turkeys could smell as well as they see and hear, we'd never kill them at all.

HISTORY OF THE TURKEY IN AMERICA

Turkeys possessed all the same acute senses 400 years ago they have now. What they hadn't yet learned was the profound distrust of people that keeps them alive today. The Pilgrims and other early settlers in North America found a promised land rich with food and game, including flocks of gullible turkeys. Thomas Morton, wrote in his 1637 book, *New English Canaan:* "Turkies there are, which divers times in great flocks have sallied by our doores; and then a gunne, being commonly in redinesse, salutes them with such a courtesie, as makes them take a turne in the Cooke roome. They daunce by the doore so well."

Although the Pilgrims ate lots of turkey and owed the birds a debt of gratitude for being dumb, plentiful, and good to eat, the turkey didn't become the traditional main course at Thanksgiving until the 1800s. Ben Franklin, incidentally, never nominated the turkey as our national symbol, either. He did, however, write a letter to his daughter, Sarah Bache, comparing turkeys favorably to eagles two years after the eagle was chosen.

Year round, unregulated hunting fed a growing, westward-moving population throughout the seventeenth, eighteenth, and nineteenth centuries. Overshooting and widespread clearing of the eastern primeval forest wiped turkeys out of New England. As settlement moved west, turkeys disappeared. The last turkey was seen in Massachusetts in 1851; in Ohio in 1878; in Iowa in 1907.

Turkeys in the West fared little better than eastern birds. In his book *A Trip to Indian Territory with General P. H. Sheridan,* General William E. Strong tells of a nighttime roost shoot in Kansas shortly after the Civil War. The hunters stole under a huge flock of roosted turkeys in the darkness and opened fire with shotguns and rifles. Strong wrote: "The firing began in earnest after my first shot, and grew into such a cannonade as I never heard before or since on a hunting field. We killed and brought to bag nineteen fine turkeys, I judge as many more were brought down from the trees badly wounded or killed outright, but which we failed to find, owing to the darkness...."

By 1900, fewer than 100,000 turkeys survived in the United States, most of them in inaccessible swamps and forests of Pennsylvania and

Wild-turkey release in Washington state. Trap-and-transfer programs have restored turkeys to 49 states. *Photo by Julia C. McClellan.*

the Southeast. Laws banning the sale of game were passed early in the twentieth century. With the birds gone and much of their habitat cleared, however, it seemed unlikely the turkey would ever return.

RESTORATION

Turkey populations hit all-time lows between 1900 and 1930. Abandoned farms began to revert to forest. The Pittman–Robertson excise tax of 1937 on sporting goods and ammunition generated funds for wildlife restoration. Early attempts to trap and transfer turkeys began in the thirties and forties.

Meanwhile, the Commonwealth of Pennsylvania experimented with releasing game farm turkeys. Blessed with remnant flocks of wild birds and huge expanses of inaccessible mountainous habitat, the Game Department established a state turkey hatchery in 1929. Pennsylvania game protectors collected wild eggs and brought them to the hatchery. Without wild hens to raise them in the woods, however, game farm turkeys had low survival rates in the wild.

The first shot in the successful war to restore the wild turkey was fired in South Carolina's Francis Marion National Forest in 1951 when a battery of blackpowder cannons launched a net over a flock of turkeys pecking at a pile of bait. The cannon net finally gave wildlife managers the ability to trap large numbers of turkeys at once.

Since 1951, trap and transfer efforts have succeeded beyond anyone's wildest imaginings: By 1999, there were 4 million turkeys nationwide.

The turkey's recent successes in proliferating are due in part to the nonprofit National Wild Turkey Federation (NWTF) founded in 1973. One hundred eighty thousand members strong, the NWTF (770 Augusta Rd., Edgefield, S.C. 29824) provides turkeys and turkey hunters with a strong voice. The NWTF has raised and spent over $90 million on restoration, research, and habitat projects over the last 25 years.

Target 2000, a cooperative initiative between the NWTF and state and federal wildlife agencies aims to restore birds to all 60 million remaining acres of turkey-suitable habitat by the century's end. Currently, 49 states hold hunting seasons. We have only ourselves to blame for the near eradication of this wonderful and very American bird. Happily, we also have ourselves to congratulate for its return. With the strict regulation of sport hunting, and the turkey's ability to give us hunters the slip on a leveled playing field, we won't run out of turkeys again.

Turkey Calls

THE TURKEY that would be the first gobbler I ever tagged sat roosted in a short mulberry tree on the bank of the Iowa River, gobbling, on average, at least three times a minute. Sitting in the mud 100 yards from his tree, I worked the diaphragm call up to the roof of my suddenly dry mouth and called timidly. *"Cluck ... cluck ...cluck?"* I ventured.

Deafening silence followed. There was no response from the mulberry tree. Even the cardinals, geese, and wood ducks seemed to stop calling and stare at me. After an interminable few seconds, the turkey gobbled. The woods came back to life. I let out the breath I was holding.

Fifteen minutes later, I worked up the nerve to call again. This time the turkey answered right back. Not long after, he jumped off the branch and, to my amazement, came to me. "What ever did I say to him?" I wondered as he closed the distance between us.

Good scouting kills probably more turkeys than good calling, but talking to the animals à la Dr. Dolittle is, nonetheless, the essence of turkey hunting. The only way you will ever learn to call turkeys is to go hunting and make some noise. Like me, you may get lucky long before you have any idea what you're doing.

(If you're a complete beginner in need of step-by-step calling instructions, put this book down and buy a video on turkey calling. You'll be able to see and hear for yourself how calls work much better than I could ever tell you in print. Then come back and read the rest of this chapter.)

The more types of callers you know how to use, the more versatile and more successful you'll be in your hunting. All calls work some of the time, none of them work all of the time, and no one knows which one will fire up a certain gobbler on a particular day.

Popular turkey calls include the slate, made of either slate or glass; the box call; and the pushbutton box. *Photo Courtesy of Outlaw Decoys.*

Case in point: a roosted creek-bottom gobbler I set upon a few years ago. I had my favorite call with me, a Lynch World Champion box, as well as a triple-reeded diaphragm call in my mouth. To any discerning ear, one sounded exactly like a turkey, the other sounded, well, like me blowing a mouth call. Guess which call the gobbler liked? The sweetest, most lifelike yelps on the Lynch box provoked the stoniest silence from the roosted bird. The slightest squeak on the mouth call, however, and he'd go berserk. It took 10 or 15 minutes to reel him in after flydown, and he ignored the box and gobbled to the diaphragm every step of the way. Go figure.

Turkey calls are inexpensive, they're fun to fool with, and you really never can have too many. Here's a rundown of the various types, with commentary provided by Matt Morrett of Hunter's Specialties and Brad Harris of Lohman Game Calls, two well-known experts.

DIAPHRAGM CALLS

The original diaphragm calls, made from jasmine leaves or dogwoods, were used both by the Indians and early settlers. With the

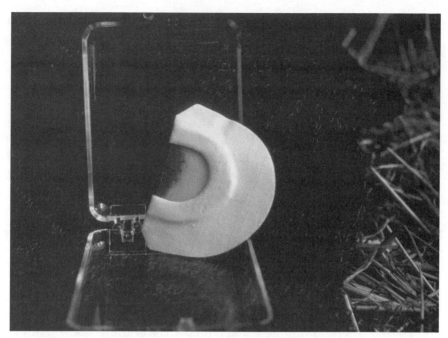

The diaphragm call takes practice to master, but it allows the hunter to make all the calls of the wild turkey without moving his hands. *Photo by Julia C. McClellan.*

invention of latex in the middle of the last century, the mouth call as we know it became possible. Today, diaphragms made from stretched latex are tremendously popular—the diaphragm being to turkey calling what the plastic worm is to bass fishing. Beginning hunters soon learn, however, that the mouth call is difficult to master.

"If you're learning the diaphragm, don't rush," advises Morrett. "Too many people try to make turkey sounds right away and develop bad habits they never unlearn. At first, just concentrate on getting comfortable with the call in your mouth. Then, work on making a single clear note. When you can do that, you've got it made."

Pick a single-reed or thin double-reeded call to start with if you've never blown a mouth call before. It's much easier to get that all-important first clear sound out of a call with only one or two thin reeds. Trust me: After a few days' practice, you won't even be aware of the ticklish, buzzing sensation you feel in the roof of your mouth when you first blow a call. Learn to carry the diaphragm between cheek and gum. That way, it won't lodge in your throat when you trip and fall in the woods. With a little practice you can flip it with your tongue from your cheek to the roof of your mouth.

With practice, you can make every vocalization of the wild turkey with a diaphragm. More important, you can do it while remaining motionless. "Also," says Harris, "if you hold your cupped hand by your mouth and turn your head, you can throw your sound effectively. I've had turkeys walk right by me toward the spot I've thrown my calls."

Morrett agrees: "I never call right at a turkey. If he hears the sound coming from one spot, it's easy for him to pinpoint your position and see you. I'll move the sound around and keep the bird guessing where the call is coming from."

While thick-reeded, extra-raspy, old-hen-type calls are popular with many hunters, both Morrett and Harris prefer high-pitched calls.

"I think turkeys hear high pitches better and respond to them more readily," says Morrett. "I used to keep wild turkeys in a pen. We lived near a firehouse, and that high-pitched whistle would really get the toms going in the spring."

Harris says he often uses single-reed calls in the woods: "They're easy to blow and they produce high-pitched calls that make birds respond. I always carry two or three others, though, because I want to be able to give the turkey the sound he wants to hear."

You can prolong the life of your mouth calls by storing them in a cool, dark place—refrigerators are perfect—in the off-season. Some hunters stick flat toothpicks between the reeds to prevent them from sticking together.

Box Calls

Although Harris is skillful enough with a diaphragm to have won Missouri state calling titles, he uses a box call 85 percent of the time.

"I started calling in 1970 with a box my grandpa made for me, and I've used boxes ever since," he says. "Now, in the video age, I can watch turkeys on tape and really study the way birds react to calling. From what I've seen, it's easier to fire a bird up to a high level of intensity with a box call."

The box is a versatile instrument that can be played several ways. "I don't turn it upside down like so many callers do; that creates too

Even calling experts like Brad Harris rely on the easy-to-use box call. *Photo courtesy of Outland Sports.*

much movement," says Harris. "Instead I use the thumb of the hand I hold the call in as a bumper on the lid when I cutt. I also take off the rubberbands. They restrict you too much."

"Don't squeeze the box, cradle it lightly. That gives you the high-pitched, ringing sound birds respond to."

Morrett, on the other hand, feels he has better control when he turns his box upside down, and he likes to slide his thumb along the sides to dampen the sound as birds get closer.

"I like to tone down the box, because calling too loud makes a lot of turkeys hang up," he says, "and boxes can be very loud."

Slate calls make excellent clucks and purrs. *Photo by Julia C. McClellan.*

The volume of the box call does make it a great locator call, and there's another advantage to it as well: "You lose too much of your hearing when you use a mouth call," Morrett explains. "You can hold a friction call away from your ears and hear gobbles better."

The biggest weakness of a box call is that it simply won't work when it's wet, although a few new composite and aluminum boxes will run in the rain. Morrett's solution for wooden calls is to store the box inside a Ziploc bag. "On rainy days, you can use the call right inside the bag," he notes.

Besides keeping your box call dry, you have to keep it properly chalked. Don't use white blackboard chalk; it's often mixed with wax, which, rather than increasing friction, reduces it, deadening the call's sound. If your call starts to sound tired and muffled, take a green scouring pad (never use sandpaper) and clean the chalk off the lid and lips or rails of the call, then lightly rechalk it.

You can also tune a call by tightening or loosening the screw that holds the lid on the box, thereby moving the point at which the lid touches the curved sides of the call; fool around with it and you'll find the call has a sweet spot.

SLATE CALLS

Morrett switched to a slate call in the crowded woods of his home state of Pennsylvania because he thought turkeys were getting educated to the sound of mouth calls. Today, with five World Friction Calling Championships to his credit (as well as being the first ever to win the Grand Nationals with a friction call, in 1990) he's the acknowledged master of the slate.

"I like the slate call for everything; you can call loud and tone it down, it's a very versatile call, and it will make every sound of the wild turkey but the gobble. The tone and quality is built into a friction call, so all you need to learn is the rhythm," he says.

"Most people don't know you can throw your sound with a slate call. The sound comes out the bottom, so you hold the call up and aim it in different directions. Trouble is, you can't do it when the turkey's in close."

Like many hunters, Harris reserves the slate call for soft, close-in calling. "I like the slate call for quiet clucks, purrs, and soft yelps. Late in the season, when visibility is low because of the foliage and the turkeys have been hammered with calling, I'll get in close and call sparingly, one or two quiet yelps and clucks. It's a boring way to hunt, but it's extremely effective, and the slate is the best for soft calling."

Traditional slate calls and wooden strikers don't work well in wet weather unless you take precautions. "To use a slate when it's wet," says Morrett, "really rough the call up before you head to the woods, and be sure to carry a Plexiglas striker." Use sandpaper to rough-up a glass call, a scouring pad for slate. New carbon and aluminum slates are virtually waterproof and will keep on squawking in a downpour. They also produce the high-frequency sounds that are currently popular among hunters.

Morrett ordinarily carries three strikers with him into the woods so he can vary his sound as needed.

"I like to try to mimic the sound of the hens in a particular area. Sometimes I'll even try to imitate one specific hen I've heard while scouting. I think a tom recognizes the voice of a hen he's been meeting. If you can imitate her tone and rhythm, you can call that tom."

PUSHBUTTON BOXES

The pushbutton call is the easiest of all turkey calls to use. A raw beginner can make turkey sounds on one with a few minutes' practice.

"We [at Lohman Manufacturing] sell a gun mount pushbutton that works great for close-in calling," says Harris. "It fits under the gun barrel and you work it with a string. You can have your gun shouldered and call the bird all the way in with very little motion."

"We were all taught to shut up and make the bird look for us when he gets close," continues Harris, "but there are so many turkeys in the woods today that I believe you have to keep calling or you'll lose the bird to another hen."

"Pushbuttons are good confidence builders for beginning callers," says Morrett, "but I think people worry too much about sounding perfect. Real hens don't always sound very good." He adds, "I don't carry a pushbutton call in the woods because it's too difficult to control the volume; you only have two choices: Go loud or muffle the call against your leg."

TUBES AND WINGBONES

The tube call is a mouth call utilizing a latex reed, but it doesn't go inside the hunter's mouth, as a diaphragm does. Originally, tube calls were made from snuff cans or pill bottles with part of the top cut away and a piece of latex stretched halfway across. Tubes are good calls for people who want to use a mouth call but have gag reflexes that prevent them from using a diaphragm," says Morrett.

The tube is a great call to gobble with, although gobbling is not a safe practice in many parts of the country. Tube calls are great loca-

Alex Rutledge cutts on a tube call to locate turkeys.

tors and absolutely wonderful for cutting; once you've got the hang of the tube, all it takes is a light *"tut-tut-tut-tut . . ."* and you can cutt all day.

Wingbones were known to turkey hunters in America long before the arrival of Columbus, and they're traditionally made from three bones of a hen's wing. You suck on a wingbone to make a yelp. Experienced wingbone users—and there aren't very many of them—can make turkeys gobble at long range. The wingbone is difficult to master, but Morrett says he's seen wingbones make turkeys answer when no other call would.

Add to the calls that imitate the vocalizations of the turkey two calls that imitate the sound of birds moving through the woods. Simply raking leaves with your hand makes the sound of a turkey looking for acorns. Done at the right time, raking can drive a gobbler crazy, because he knows there's a hen nearby but she won't answer his calls.

Another old trick is to use an actual dried turkey wing, flapped to sound like a bird flying down from the roost or across a creek. Even brushing the wingtip lightly against the bark of a tree can make a roosted turkey gobble early in the morning. Two manufacturers now sell wing calls, so you no longer need to shoot a fall hen to make your own.

LOCATOR CALLS

Locating a turkey by making him gobble increases your chances and boosts your confidence. Turkeys gobble at provocative sounds, and most successful hunters carry a number of locator calls.

"I've found the crow call to be my best all-around locator," says Harris. "Coyote howlers are great for western birds, and good for eastern turkeys, too."

"Don't categorize your calls by time of day," Harris advises, noting that some hunters hoot only in the morning and evening and crow-call only at midday. "Use what works no matter what time of day, and be ready to try all three [categories of calls]."

"Stick with a short, distinct series. Call too much and you'll drown out the answer."

Morrett also uses crow calls and owl hooters. "I use crow calls at midday after I've made a bird gobble with a cutt; crow calls work best when a bird's already fired up. I'll crow-call as I'm moving in on the bird so I know where he is. I don't like to use hen calls when I'm on my way to a tom; I like to get in as close as I'm going to get, then call like a hen."

Pileated-woodpecker and peacock calls work too, even in areas where there aren't any pileated woodpeckers, much less peacocks. Bear in mind that turkeys gobble to all sorts of loud noises—sirens, gunshots, foghorns, thunder—and you should always pause and listen after any loud noise in the woods to see if it's startled a bird into gobbling.

Both Morrett and Harris carry a box, a slate with multiple strikers, several mouth calls, and two or three locators with them when they go hunting. Although an arsenal of calls increases the hunter's odds, both men have spent enough time in the woods to know that some days none of them work. Says Morrett: "If there were such a thing as a foolproof turkey call, most call makers would be out of business and turkey hunting wouldn't be any fun."

To which Harris adds philosophically: "There are some turkeys I just can't call if the time isn't right, no matter what I do. The real secret of game calling is to call them when they're ready to be called."

A Dictionary of Turkey Sounds

Turkeys communicate with a wide variety of noises, most sounding like a rusty gate squeaking shut. Hunters only need to know how to yelp and perhaps cluck to succeed in the woods, but if you visit a place, it's always good to learn the language. Here's a Turkey-to-English guide of the most common sounds, and their uses by both turkeys and hunters:

Cackle (15 or 20 yelps, starts very fast, then slows): Hens often cackle loudly as they fly up and down to the roost. Some hunters imitate the cackle early in the morning while beating their hat against their leg to simulate wingbeats.

Cackling at dusk can help you locate birds by making them gobble in response. A cackle at that time also sets the stage for the next morning, since the gobbler has heard a new hen (you) close by.

Cluck (like a chicken's cluck, usually with long pauses between each cluck): Turkeys cluck when they're happy, feeding, or just walking around. It's a soft, distracted sound, as if they were humming tunelessly. Clucks let other turkeys know where they are, in a low-key way. For hunters, clucks are good calls to use when birds have been pressured with a lot of aggressive calling.

The sound is a little popping noise. When gobblers cluck, it sounds as if they've got peanut butter stuck to the roof of their mouths. You'll often hear jakes gobbler-clucking when they come to a hen call.

Cutt (Cutts are a series of fast, syncopated *puck* sounds): Cutts are a series of sharp, syncopated clucks made by excited hens. You'll hear as many as 10 or 15 fast clucks when a hen cutts. Gobblers often respond to cutting by gobbling, making the cutt an excellent locator call and a call used by "run and gun"–style hunters.

Drumming (a *ffft* sound, then a low hum): Drumming is a humming sound made by the gobbler as he struts. It's a low-frequency hum, or so I'm told. Some people, myself included, can't hear drumming turkeys at all, no matter how close by they may be. Others can hear toms drum 100 yards away and, since turkeys will often strut without gobbling, it's a real advantage to learn to recognize the sound.

Gobbling (sounds like a high-pitched *Gil-obble-obble-obble;* hard to mistake for anything else): Turkeys actually gobble year round. Male turkeys gobble to assert dominance over one another, to stake out territories, to attract hens, and as a reflex, or "shock gobble."

Most gobbling occurs on the roost, especially in the morning but sometimes in the evening as well. Merriam's and Rio Grandes gobble all day long and generally more often than do easterns.

Some hunters will gobble at dominant gobblers to challenge them during the hunt or to locate them on the roost either in the morning or the evening. For safety's sake, always remember that the gobble call makes you sound exactly like the bird other hunters are trying to shoot; then decide if you really think it's a good idea to gobble at that time and place.

Kee Kee (three to five shrill whistles, sounds like *hurry, hurry, hurry*): Known as the whistle, it's a poult's attempt at a yelp. The high-pitched series of whistles, sometimes followed by a few yelps, is a very important call in the fall after you've broken up a flock.

Purr (a trilled *trrrrr* sound; turkeys often make several short purrs): Purrs, like clucks, are primarily contentment noises. Turkeys will cluck and purr about happily as they feed. Turkeys also purr loudly when they're angry, and gobblers will purr as they posture before and during a fight. Quiet clucking and purring works well on pressured birds.

So-called "fighting purrs" can bring gobblers in exactly the same way rattling horns attract whitetails.

Putt (sounds like *Putt!* or *pert!;* a short and explosive sound; turkeys usually make just one or two): Turkeys putt when they're nervous. A bird that's spotted danger—say, you, with a gun—will become quite agitated and putt. Beginning hunters live in terror of accidentally making the alarm putt, which differs only from the cluck in intensity. Don't worry about it; if you make a sound you think is a putt, just throw in some quiet clucks or purrs.

Some hunters will putt loudly on purpose to make a turkey come out of strut and stick his head up for a clear shot.

Yelps: (*yawk, yawk, yawk,* often a series of five to eight yelps): Along with the cluck, the yelp is the basic turkey noise. Hunters used to call hen yelps "love yelps" because they are the primary sound hens make to gobblers in the spring. Hens also yelp to gather their young. Gobblers yelp, too. Gobbler yelps are lower-pitched, coarser, and slower than hen yelps. If a gobbler yelps back to your calls, he may have mistaken you for a gobbler that wants to fight.

If you learn no other call, you can end up killing plenty of turkeys simply by yelping at them first.

CHAPTER

3

Turkey Guns

"**S**HOOT HIM when you can," the guide whispered into my ear. No better time than the present: The gobbler stood just 25 yards away, his white head nearly glowing in the pale morning light.

The gun boomed. The turkey flew.

I had always wondered how people managed to miss wild turkeys. Now I know. Aim too high, jerk the trigger, raise your head, he's gone. A standing turkey should be a sitting duck, yet hunters miss gobblers much more often than you'd think.

Shooting turkeys into their bodies with big pellets cripples birds, and many states have banned the use of shot larger than No. 4 for safety reasons. Instead, you need to swarm a turkey's head and neck with a cloud of small pellets, relying on three or more of them to strike the brain or vertebrae.

TURKEY GUN CHOICES

Countless turkeys have fallen to long-barreled, full-choked duck guns over the years; however, most serious hunters shoot specialized turkey guns. Some like the simplicity of pumps, others prefer the recoil reduction of an autoloader. Since rate of fire doesn't matter in turkey hunting, a few hunters choose bolt actions or even single shots. What sets these guns apart? Three or three-and-a-half-inch 12-gauge chambers; short barrels for easier handling; supertight turkey-gun choke tubes; matte or camo finishes; and sling swivels. Most come with iron sights or are drilled and tapped for scope mounts. All

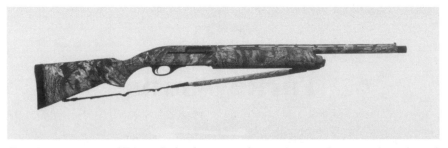

This Remington 11-87 has all the features of a modern turkey gun: short barrel, extra-full choke, magnum chamber, front and middle beads, camo finish and a sling. *Photo courtesy of Remington.*

the major manufacturers now make a turkey model of almost any pump or auto in their line.

SIGHTS

At 20 yards, some turkey chokes jam almost 100 percent of the pellets into a clump so small you can cover it with both hands. Placing tight patterns effectively requires sights more sophisticated than a single plain bead. Not only will sights let you aim your pattern accurately, they can compensate for a barrel that doesn't shoot straight. I once owned an Auto-5 that shot so high I had to aim at a gobbler's toes to hit him in the head. A set of adjustable Williams "Slugger" sights on the rib made that gun into a fine turkey shooter.

If your gun has a front and middle bead, you at least have the benefit of two sights to align. However, iron sights, peeps, red dots, and even scopes work much better.

The newest aftermarket sights, by Tru-Glo, Hi-Viz, and others, feature fiber-optic beads that show up extremely well in low light. As of this writing, some Remington and Winchester guns were available with factory-equipped fiber-optic sights. The venerable Williams peep sight affords an even better view of the target than do iron sights. Just unscrew the rear disk and aim through the threaded aperture for quicker target acquisition early in the morning.

Battery-operated red-dot sights such as the Aimpoint appear on

A low-power scope can help you accurately place the tight patterns of modern turkey chokes. *Photo by Julia C. McClellan.*

more turkey guns every year. Instead of crosshairs, these no-power scopes feature a bright red aiming dot. They're great early in the morning and extremely quick any time of day. If you choose a red-dot model, pick one with a large aiming dot. Dots are measured in minutes of angle (MOA). A 5 MOA dot, for instance, covers 5 inches at 100 yards. For turkey hunting, look for a dot in the 10 to 15 MOA size; it will show up much better than the smaller 1 to 5 MOA dots popular with handgun shooters.

When shopping for scopes, consider something in the 1 to 2.5x range. Several specialty turkey scopes have "circle-plexes" to help you

Modern turkey loads pack as much shot into a 12-gauge hull as old-time market hunters loaded into their 8-bores. *Photo by Julia C. McClellan.*

estimate range. These are regular crosshairs with a circle the size of a shot pattern at 40 yards, superimposed.

There are a number of aftermarket, no-gunsmithing mounts available from B-Square and other manufacturers for most pumps and autos if you want to mount a scope or red-dot sight to your gun. Several varieties of aftermarket iron sights and fiber-optic beads either clamp onto the rib of the gun or stick to it with powerful magnets.

Turkey Loads

The more pellets you sling at a turkey's head, the better your chances of putting two or three into his brain. In recent years, manufacturers have learned to cram up to 2¼ ounces of shot into 12-gauge hulls. In truth, the old 2¾-inch 1½-ounce magnums kill turkeys extremely well.

Turkey loads and chokes can swarm a gobbler's head and neck with multiple hits for clean kills. *Photo courtesy of Winchester.*

The new stuff kills them deader (if that's possible), albeit at a hefty price in increased recoil. Nos. 4, 5, and 6 shot remain the most popular sizes. They have adequate energy to penetrate skulls and vertebrae, yet their pellet counts are high enough to ensure good pattern density.

Regardless of what load you choose, you need to pattern your gun. Look for a shell that at your maximum range prints at least 16 hits above the feather line on your paper turkey-head target. Sixteen hits should ensure at least three hits in the skull and neck vertebrae. Briley Manufacturing's Chuck Webb says his company arrived at the 16:3 formula after shooting thousands of rounds at turkey-head targets while developing their turkey chokes.

Even the same box of 10 shells can produce surprising variation from one shot pattern to the next. Don't shoot one pattern and assume that's how your gun prints a particular load. Instead shoot, 3-, 5-, or even 10-shot strings to get a real idea of how your gun and choke perform.

PRACTICE

Outside of shooting a couple of test patterns, few hunters actually practice with their turkey guns. It pays to run a couple of boxes of shells through your gun, shooting paper turkey-head targets from various distances. Take a few shots while you're twisting around a tree. If you're right-handed, try some left-handed shots. It's very difficult for a right-hander to twist and shoot to his or her right side. You'll find it's much easier to switch shoulders without spooking a bird than it is to scoot all the way around the tree to get a bead on a turkey that sneaks in from your right.

Concentrate on keeping your cheek on the stock. When you aim at a turkey target, don't hold on the head. Instead, pick a point halfway down the neck. The center of your pattern will strike the neck while the top half hits the head. If you shoot high, there's a good chance you'll drop the bird with a head shot anyway. Also, with a midneck hold, you're less likely to miss if the turkey suddenly moves his head.

Do your shoulder and wallet a favor and practice with light trap loads. Just be sure to try a few magnums before the season to make absolutely certain they shoot to the same point of impact.

ESTIMATING RANGE

You can rely on most standard full chokes to kill turkeys cleanly at 30 yards and a step or two more. Superfull turkey chokes add 8 to 10 yards to your effective range.

Regardless of your choke choice, accurate range estimation is critical to good turkey shooting. Even the dense patterns of the superfull chokes loosen up quickly after a certain point. At long range, a few yards can make the difference between a sure-kill cluster and a patchy, marginal spread.

Since turkeys are big birds, lots of hunters underestimate range. To many people, a gobbler always looks closer than it really is. More than one southerner, accustomed to hunting 18-pound gobblers at home, has come up to the Midwest and seriously miscalculated the range on our waddling 25-pounders, shooting far too soon.

A West Virginia hunter told me last spring about watching through his new 4x scope as a bird came in. He waited until it looked as big as a Holstein in the crosshairs, then shot, only to find that in real-life 1x vision the bird was still 75 yards away.

Rather than judging range by the size of the turkey, you're better off picking range markers—trees, rocks, bushes—in a circle 30 yards away from your setup. Practice your range-estimating skills by picking objects in your backyard or on the sidewalk, guessing the range, then pacing off the distance. If you can't learn to estimate yardage fairly accurately, take a bowhunter's rangefinder into the woods. Choose a model like the Ranging R-60 Sureshot that accurately measures short distances, say, from 10 to 60 yards.

Finally, although closer is usually better, optimum shooting range at turkeys lies between 20 and 30 yards, where your pattern has an opportunity to open up a little. Let turkeys come into range, but don't let them sit in your lap.

Making the Shot

If you're right-handed, sit with your back to a tree, facing slightly to the right of where you expect the turkey to appear. Draw both knees up, rest the receiver of your gun on your knees, and tuck the butt lightly under your arm. (A padded sling, incidentally, can double as a gun rest to keep the sharp steel edges of the receiver from digging into your knee.) Ideally, you'll have to do nothing more than ease the gun forward and lower your face onto the stock when you're ready to shoot. With the gun balanced on your knee, you'll have a good solid shooting position, and one you can easily hold while waiting for the right moment to shoot. Try to move only when the turkey is behind a tree trunk or brush pile and can't spot you. Just before the shot, some hunters make a single alarm putt to make the bird stop and raise his head.

After you shoot, run to the bird quickly, and stand on his neck until he's done thrashing. Pick up a dead turkey while he's still kicking and you risk a nasty spurring. Every once in a while, your pattern may miss the brain and vertebrae but sever an artery instead. In that case, a fatally hit bird may run or fly off. Always assume you've hit any turkey you've shot at, and make a careful search for the body.

BLACKPOWDER SHOTGUNS, RIFLES, AND BOWS

Although most hunters carry pump or autoloading shotguns into the woods, you might someday choose to hunt with a rifle (where legal), a bow, or a blackpowder shotgun.

Rifles

Despite the heritage of Colonial turkey shoots and Sergeant York, rifles are fading from modern turkey hunting and today are legal in only a few states. If you do hunt turkeys with a rifle, choose one of the smaller .22s, such as the .22 rimfire magnum, .22 Hornet, .218 Bee, .222 or .223. Stay away from rapidly expanding varmint bullets, which ruin meat. Shoot a bullet that expands more moderately, or, if you're an absolute dead-eye, shoot solids and place them very carefully.

Try to shoot your bird at the base of the neck, which should result in a clean kill and little meat damage. It's an easy shot if the bird is facing right at you, trickier if he's sideways and you have to figure out where the feathers end and the turkey begins.

Bows

Luring a turkey into bow range and drawing on him without getting busted is one of toughest feats in all of hunting. That challenge motivates hunters like Will Walker of Primos Game Calls, who's hunted turkeys exclusively with a bow for 10 years.

Walker reduces his draw weight from 70 pounds down to 50 to 55 pounds when he switches from deer to turkeys. "It's easier for me to hold the bow at full draw," he says. "When you turkey-hunt, your muscles stiffen from long periods of sitting still."

Lately, Walker has changed over to expandable broadheads that stay in the turkey's body when the arrow strikes. Accuracy, he

Will Walker with a Florida gobbler. Walker reduces the draw on his compound from 70 pounds to 55 for turkey hunting. *Photo courtesy Primos, Inc.*

believes, should be the bowhunter's number one concern. "Shoot the broadhead you shoot most accurately," he advises.

Walker's favorite shot is broadside, at the butt of the wing. He also likes the rear-end shot when the bird is turned straight away from him. He cautions against shooting birds facing straight ahead. There's too much chance of the arrow glancing off the sternum and tearing through the breast, leaving only a deep flesh wound.

Blackpowder Shotguns

Turkey hunting being a sport in which quick reloads don't matter, many hunters find that blackpowder shotguns add the perfect touch

Author took this 22-pound Missouri gobbler with a
Modern Muzzleloading 12-gauge.

of nostalgia and extra challenge to the hunt. In truth, blackpowder
guns can be loaded to deliver such excellent patterns that they hardly
handicap the hunter at all. My Knight muzzleloading shotgun has a
screw-in extra-full tube and shoots tighter patterns than any of my
modern guns. To get the best performance from a blackpowder gun,
you'll need a plastic shotcup that will protect the pellets from defor-
mation as they travel down the bore.

I've found a shotcup designed for modern 3½-inch 12-gauge steel
reloads that fits perfectly in my gun and holds nearly 2 ounces of
shot. I load my powder, ram the shotcup into place, add shot, then
push a plastic-foam overshot wad snugly on top of the whole load.

Consult your gun's manufacturer for maximum recommended
loads. If you shoot an antique gun, talk to a good gunsmith before

experimenting with different loads. Blackpowder is a much more forgiving propellant than modern smokeless powders. Part of the fun of shooting blackpowder guns lies in the freedom you have to mix and match various components while searching for the ideal load.

Although some new muzzleloading guns can be loaded to near-modern ballistics, you'll shoot your best patterns with fairly light powder charges, which translate into lower velocities and less energy retained downrange. Knowing I have only one chance, I try to limit my shots at turkeys with blackpowder to well under 35 yards.

You pick your perfect turkey gun, learn what it can and can't do, practice, and take your chances in the woods. Realize that if you chase turkeys long enough you'll whiff some birds. Think of it as part of the fun, or, at least, cultivate a philosophical attitude. One vastly experienced and well-adjusted turkey hunter tells me he's missed 1 out of every 10 turkeys over the years. He says: "When I stop getting so excited that I never miss anymore, it'll be time to quit."

Number of pellets in selected turkey loads

SHOT SIZE:	4	5	6
1¼ ounces	169	212	281
1½ ounces	202	255	337
1⅝ ounces	219	276	366
2 ounces	270	340	450
2¼ ounces	304	382	506

CHAPTER

4

Turkey Gear

TURKEY HUNTING needn't be a gear-intensive pursuit. My first season, I carried only two mouth calls, a mesh headnet and a healthy dose of beginner's luck into the woods. I came out with a 21 1/2-pound gobbler slung over my shoulder. Nevertheless, there's a pile of accessories that will make you a more comfortable, more effective (albeit more heavily burdened) hunter. Turkey-hunting gear doesn't cost much, and sooner or later, you'll probably own two of every useful turkey-hunting widget made.

The trick to managing your turkey gear is to buy a good vest with lots of pockets. I like the strap variety, which is cool in warm weather and easy to layer over heavy clothes on cold mornings. A vest with a turkey-size gamebag is very useful for storing extra layers of clothing, as well. Before the season, load your vest with everything you deem essential. Then, when you stumble out of bed at 3:30 A.M., you just have to grab the vest and your gun and find the front door.

Do yourself a huge favor and memorize what gadget you put in which pocket. Here's what a well-stocked vest might hold:

Bug Dope: Where I live, mosquitoes don't hatch until after turkey season ends. One day in a South Carolina swamp during a record wet spring, however, convinced me to carry bug dope in my vest pocket.

Call Tuning Kit: To keep your friction calls running, you'll need chalk, a piece of scouring pad for boxes, sandpaper or scouring pad for slates, and a plastic bag to protect your calls on rainy days. A few years ago I bought a commercially made tuning kit from Quaker Boy that fit into a snuff box.

39

Author fishes a box call from the pockets of his vest. A good vest will keep your gear accessible and organized all season long.

Compact Binoculars: Is that a turkey or a stump? Binoculars are especially useful for spotting turkeys in fields.

Compass/GPS (Global Positioning System): For marking roost trees, strut zones, dust baths, and for finding your way back to the truck. Don't leave home without 'em.

Cushion: As important as calls, maybe more so, since if you sit still in the right place long enough, you'll kill turkeys. Some hunters carry low folding chairs or camp stools into the woods.

Extra Gloves and Headnet: As one who's always losing gloves in mysterious ways, I keep two pairs of camo gloves and an extra head-net in my vest.

Extra Shells: Unless you get in a war with the turkeys, three or four shells should be enough.

First Aid: At the very least, carry Band-Aids in your wallet and per-haps a few aspirins in a film can.

Flashlight: Essential for finding stuff you drop in the dark and pick-ing your way through tangled woods.

Knife/Multitool: A zillion uses in the woods, from tuning box calls with the screwdriver to field-dressing turkeys with the blade.

Mouth Call Caddy: Mine is by Hunter's Specialties. It looks like a lit-tle wallet for mouth calls and holds half a dozen diaphragms. It also has a neck lanyard, which I tie to one strap of my vest.

Orange Cap: Wear it as you walk and call or when you carry your bird out of the woods.

Pocket Camera: It's much better to take your "hero shots" in the glo-rious spring woods than at home in the yard, with clothesline run-ning behind you and the kid's Big Wheel in the background.

Pruning Shears: A small pair of shears lets you quickly and quietly clear a space to sit and swing your gun barrel.

Snack: Why hunt hungry? A granola bar and a juice box provide just the sugar boost I need to stay in the field at midmorning.

Rain Gear: Turkeys gobble well on drizzly days and go nuts when they hear thunder. Keep a poncho or compact rainsuit in your game-bag, and stay in the woods.

Warm Hat: It's true: "If your feet are cold, put on a hat." A knit watch cap fits much more easily in a vest pocket than does an extra pair of boots.

CLOTHES

Turkey-hunting clothes should be quiet and camouflaged. I like cool ripstop cotton garments, with warmer clothing layered on top.

Which camo pattern? They're all good. Frankly, few of the top hunters I've been with obsess about camo patterns. They wear camo, but they rely on woodsmanship to keep themselves hidden. Pick something that blends with the predominant colors of your area, and concentrate on sitting still, not silhouetting yourself, and on staying in the shadows.

Most important, both from a stealth and safety standpoint, avoid gaps in your camo. An expanse of bare wrist, say, might look like a bobbing turkey neck to another hunter and be a warning flag to a turkey. By the same token, pick a cap with a long bill that throws a shadow over your eyes.

Buy gloves with long, knit wrists and pants with enough length to cover your lower legs when you sit with your knees drawn up. Wear a face mask that doesn't expose a lot of shiny forehead or ruddy cheek. I like the three-quarter style that pulls down around my neck when not in use.

Turkey hunters walk, often through muck, sometimes through snakes, and usually for miles and miles. You'll hunt turkeys in temperatures ranging from the twenties to the eighties. I wear tall rubber boots with Air-Bob soles about 90 percent of the time, because they're comfortable and I don't hunt where I need to scramble up and down rocky bluffs. For many folks, early in the season, insulated leather boots or even Sorel-type felt packs (some of the new models are pretty good walking boots) may prove to be comfortable choices.

As the weather warms, uninsulated leather boots or rubber-footed "Bean Boots" are all you need in the woods. Don't neglect the new breed of "light hikers," which are crosses between traditional hiking boots and running shoes. Although not marketed directly to hunters, these are lightweight boots made for walking all day in the woods, which just happens to be what we hunters do. Of course, if you hunt in snake country, your needs change. Both Rocky and Russell make tall, lightweight, camouflaged snakeproof boots for turkey hunters.

Whatever boots you choose, you're wasting your money if you

wear them with cheap white gym socks that quickly soak with sweat. Combine a thin pair of polypropylene liner socks and wool outer socks to wick moisture away from your feet and keep them dry and comfortable.

BLINDS

Most of the time, you don't need a blind to hunt turkeys; you just need to sit still. However, if you plan to stake out a field edge for a few hours or set up and call where you've seen birds, a blind makes the interminable wait much easier to tolerate. Many bowhunters rely on blinds to conceal the movement of drawing their bow. As a gun hunter, I usually don't use a blind, but for long vigils (for my gnatlike attention span, that means anything over 45 minutes) I like a low blind that stakes into the ground and hides my fidgeting hands and feet. I use a Hunter's Specialties "Super-Light" portable blind that

Blinds, like this one from Hunter's Specialties, allow hunters to fidget a little during long waits. *Photo by Julia C. McClellan.*

stakes out in seconds, and rolls up just as quickly. It weighs very little and goes with me everywhere whether I use it or not. Some hunters cache blinds and decoys in the brush at strategic spots in their hunting areas. Of course, you can always build a makeshift blind from branches and brush if you have a pair of clippers. Just a few branches in front of you will do wonders in breaking up your outline. The hard part will be remembering what vest pocket you put your clippers in.

CHAPTER

Scouting

S HROUDED BY the early morning darkness, I eased into a hollow in the trunk of an old locust tree that seemed to have been shaped with a turkey hunter's back in mind. Propping the shotgun on my knees, I waited and watched the sun rise, the gobbler 100 yards to my front sounding off so regularly as to almost become monotonous. Two hundred yards behind me, I heard the hen wake up and begin to yelp softly. The gobbler answered her. I clucked, he gobbled. Short story made even shorter: He hopped off the branch and strutted right in, gobbling to every call I made.

Even world champions will admit that the best way to be a good caller is to sit where the turkey wants to go. Put in your time scouting before the season, and you greatly increase the odds that your hunt will be a quick and happy one. I'd begun scouting that particular gobbler long before opening day. I knew where he roosted, and I knew where he went to meet his hens in the morning. I'd learned to find my way quickly into the woods in the dark, and I even had a comfortable tree picked out to sit against.

Turkey scouting often begins months before the spring season opens and lasts right up until the night before a hunt.

FALL AND WINTER: WHERE THE BIRDS ARE

You can start looking for places to hunt spring gobblers during deer season, with the following caveat: Good spring turkey habitat may hold no turkeys in the fall. Occasionally, you'll see turkeys in the fall

Steve Puppe glasses the Black Hills for Merriam's turkeys. A high vantage point like this one makes a good place to listen for gobbling, too. *Photo by Julia C. McClellan.*

in places where you won't find them come spring. Although eastern wild turkey don't migrate like Merriam's, they may move up to 2 or 3 miles from their winter to their spring range. Merriam's turkeys may travel 30 or 40 miles in the spring as they migrate from low to high elevations.

So, rather than looking for turkeys, look for good habitat. Turkeys were once thought to be birds of the big woods, but in fact ideal habitat for easterns includes a mix of mast-bearing hardwoods and clearings. Turkeys love pastures and hayfields; gobblers like to strut where they can be seen, while poults rely on the ready supply of insects they find in the grassy fields.

LATE WINTER, EARLY SPRING: SETTING THE STAGE

The more familiar you are with the terrain you hunt, the better your chances of calling toms into range. I've wasted plenty of time trying to call up turkeys that were, unbeknownst to me, on the far side of impassable obstacles, including, once, a golf course.

Buy a U.S. Geological Survey quadrangle map of your hunting area (write to: USGS Map Sales, Box 25286, Denver, CO 80225, or call 1–800–USA–MAPS). These topographic maps show elevations, water sources, and timbered areas. Carry a pocket notebook on scouting trips to record features of interest, then copy your notes onto your topo map at home. Mark creeks, sloughs, steep draws, brush piles, fences, and anything else that may prevent a turkey from coming to your call. A GPS unit is ideal for this type of scouting, as you can record the location of features of interest on the GPS, then transfer them to your map later. By studying the map before and after trips to your hunting grounds, you'll build a detailed picture of the area in your mind.

Now is also the time to learn your way around the woods so you won't get lost in the dark. Look for landmarks you can recognize before dawn, and memorize the location of that old strand of barbwire that stretches across the trail.

SPRING: FINDING AND PATTERNING TURKEYS

As the season approaches, the hens will gravitate toward nesting spots, and the toms will begin to stake out their territories and gobble. You'll probably hear more gobbling in the weeks before the season begins than at any other time of the spring; birds will sound off all day as they challenge one another and fight. Now, with the birds easy to locate, you can begin looking and listening for actual turkeys to hunt.

Scouting is really pretty simple; just keep your eyes and ears open. As Hunter's Specialties Pro Ray Eye told me once: "Six weeks before the season comes in, you'll hear a bird start to gobble, then another one will answer a quarter-mile away. The gobbles get louder and louder as the birds get closer together. You'll hear a terrible fight, and the squirrels and jays and crows will all go nuts. Then the woods go quiet, and you'll hear one bird gobbling back to where he started. I make a note, *Here's where I'm going to hunt.*"

A gobbler's primary feathers can measure up to 18 inches.

Gobblers are big birds, and they leave big sign: 18-inch primaries, 4½-inch footprints, long, J-shaped droppings. Scratches in the leaves near mast trees tell you where turkeys have been feeding. Look for drag marks left by the wingtips of strutting gobblers; in dirt or sand they look like a mark you might make by spreading your fingertips and dragging them on the ground. Mark areas where you find plenty of sign on your topo map.

Piles of droppings beneath the branches of a tree indicate a roost. Although turkeys do not always roost in exactly the same tree, they often use the same general area. Turkeys prefer a hardwood with sturdy, horizontal branches as a roost, but I've seen them spend the night in all kinds of trees, including near-saplings no more than 10 feet tall.

Once you've determined where the turkeys are, you can start to pattern a few birds. Get out in the woods at dawn and listen for gob-

Turkeys leave big sign. A gobbler's footprints measure 4 to 4½ inches long.

bling. Note the direction a tom travels after flying down; he's probably on his way to meet his hens in a particular spot. Glass open fields later on in the morning, and you may see him strutting and gobbling at the same time and place every day, too. Learn his routine, and you can be waiting for him.

THE NIGHT BEFORE: ROOSTING A TOM

The final step in preseason scouting is to roost a bird the night before a hunt. At dusk, listen for gobblers gobbling on the roost, hens cackling as they fly up, and the unforgettable sound of huge wings lifting 20-pound bodies into the air.

Crow, coyote, owl and gobble calls will make roosting toms gobble, as will a gobble call. Some hunters like to imitate the fly-up cackle of a hen, both to provoke a gobble and on the theory that the turkey will come looking for the "hen" the next morning. If turkeys roost close to your position, wait until full darkness before leaving the area. The next day, arrive well before first light, and set up near the roost in the direction you believe the bird will travel. Roosting a bird is far from a sure thing if you don't have an idea which way he plans to go in the morning. If you have to guess, try to set up between the roost and the nearest open area where the turkey may go to strut. Although conventional wisdom says you should try to call a bird downhill, I've seen turkeys fly down from hillsides and head straight for the creek bottoms to strut in the flats.

Although many successful hunters are happy only if they have several turkeys patterned before the season begins (so they have backups in case someone else shoots "their" bird), any scouting you can do is better than no scouting at all. One year I didn't bother visiting my favorite river-bottom timber until opening morning, only to find my prime hunting spot under 3 feet of fast-moving water.

At the very least, you should know if you need to build an ark.

CHAPTER

The Dawn Patrol

L EANING BACK against the tree trunk, I've got the best seat in the house this morning. All around me crows caw, owls hoot, geese honk, cardinals call "fierce, fierce." A raccoon scuttles past on his way home to bed after a night's foraging. Cock pheasants sound off so close by I can hear their wingbeats as they stretch and crow like barnyard roosters. Every few minutes, the electric gobble of the turkey slices through the din in the busy timber: He's right where I left him last night, in the branches of a maple tree 100 yards up the creek bottom.

Straining my ears for the *woofing* of huge wings, I yelp quietly on the slate as soon as the turkey flies down. The tom gobbles back immediately. I answer, and he gobbles again 10 seconds later, the sound telling me he's closing the distance between us rapidly.

The tom first rolls into view atop a bank 45 yards away. He's blown himself up like a beachball and tilted his fan to catch the soft dawn light. He manages to look both majestic and faintly ridiculous at the same time, as only a strutting turkey can. The bird follows a deer trail down the bank, stepping daintily as if trying to negotiate stairs in heels and a hoopskirt. Once inside gun range, he obligingly stops, deflates, and looks around. The crash of the 12-gauge silences the morning woods, save for the thrashing of the bird in the leaves.

And that is how classic early-morning turkey hunting is supposed to go. You slip into the predawn woods and sit up against a tree 100 to 200 yards from a roosted gobbler. On the limb the turkey gobbles to owls, crows, other turkeys, the sunrise. He answers your calls, then flies down from his roost about the time the sun cracks the horizon. He struts into gun range, interrupting your every yelp with an eager gobble. When you put your tag on his leg, it's still at least an hour too early to call all your friends and tell them you've got a turkey.

While I've shot most of my gobblers before 6:30 in the morning, the magic hour at dawn isn't always the easiest time to bag a bird. Toms gobble hard early in the morning, so you know where they are. On the other hand, that gobbler often knows right where he's going first thing in the morning, and you're also faced with competition from real hens.

FINDING A TURKEY

If you haven't roosted a turkey the night before the hunt, you need to be up on a ridgetop or in an open field listening for turkeys to crank up in the morning.

The old advice was, that first gobble may be the only one you hear all morning, so get to it immediately. Hunters crashed through the darkened woods after the faintest gobble, ran up and down steep ridges, and forded icy streams to reach distant toms. Having grown up spoiled in an era of many turkeys, I wait until I think all the turkeys are awake and gobbling, then take my pick.

Although turkeys will gobble to crow calls, coyote calls, and owl hoots in the morning, it's often better to stay quiet and let them start on their own if possible so you don't alert them to your presence. Just because a bird gobbles—which he does out of reflex— doesn't mean he thinks a sound is natural. You could probably locate turkeys by yelling "Hey!" but you wouldn't kill very many of them.

Once you've started on your way to the bird, however, hoot- or crow-call as you move through the woods, both to pinpoint the location of the bird and to make sure there aren't other, closer turkeys around. One of my fondest turkey-hunting memories is of standing in the dark at the edge of a woodlot with Ray Eye, preparing to move in on a bird we'd heard gobble once. We held the following whispered conversation:

RAY (gesturing to a spot 50 yards away): Do you think we need to get over to that next ridge?

Many hunters try to set up above gobblers and call them uphill.

ME: I don't know Ray, he sounded pretty close to me.

RAY: I'll just hoot once. (Hoots softly.)

FIVE TURKEYS: (all within 50 to 75 yards): *Gobble, Gobble, Gobble, Gobble, Gobble, Gobble, Gobble, Gobble, Gobble, Gobble.*

RAY: (pauses, as if carefully pondering our next move): I think we should sit right here.

ME: (trying hard not to laugh out loud): You're the guide, Ray.

Twenty minutes later I put my tag on a 23-pound bird.

How close you set up to a tom in the morning can make the difference between success and sitting in the woods. M.A.D. Calls's Mark Drury likes to roost turkeys the night before a hunt, then sneak in well before dawn to sit within 60 yards of the bird.

"Once I started roosting birds and getting in tight on them the next morning, my success rate jumped way up," he says. "If you can get close and set up on the uphill side, when he flies down he'll

Flapping a wing in the morning to simulate a flying hen is an effective call.

almost be in gun range. All you have to do is convince him to walk a few yards in your direction."

Drury's approach has its risks; if you get too close to a bird, he might spot you, ending the hunt before it begins. I try to find a spot between 100 and 200 yards from a roosted turkey. Early in the season, when the branches are bare, a turkey in a tree can see a long way at first light. As the trees leaf out, however, you often can sneak to within 100 yards fairly easily.

Traditionally, hunters try to call either from above or from the same level or contour as the turkey. Follow that advice when you can, but always remember that it's more important to set up along the turkey's line of travel first thing in the morning. Ideally, you've scouted the bird and you know which way he goes after flydown. Usually, he'll head out to strut right away, so position yourself between the roost and an open field, creek bottom, ridgetop logging road, or oak flat.

Take a minute to clear a comfortable place to sit when you set up; you may be there awhile.

CALLING

Most hunters begin the morning hunt with a quiet, sleepy tree yelp, calling only once while the tom is in the tree. All you want to do is let him know where you are. He may gobble back, but even if he doesn't answer, you can be certain he's heard you. Even the tips of a turkey wing brushed against a tree trunk are enough to let a gobbler know there's a hen nearby. Wait until the tom flies down before yelping excitedly.

If he interrupts your calls, gobbling while you're in midyelp, keep calling; he's definitely interested. At the same time, if a gobbling turkey falls silent, don't assume right away that he's lost interest. Resist the temptation to crank him back up with the call. Instead, get your gun ready. When turkeys shut up, it often means they're on the way to you.

There are two schools of thought when it comes to calling turkeys: Some think less is more, others believe more is more. Neither school is right all the time. The first calling advice I ever heard was: "Yelp three times and shut up." That's old-school thinking, but it's still valid today. Call sparingly, scratch your hand in the leaves occasionally, and make the turkey come looking for you.

In many parts of the country, however, you'll face a problem old-time hunters never knew: too many turkeys. Call too little, new-breed hunters say, and you lose out to real hens. As hunting pro Eddie Salter puts it: "My theory is, a lot of times you call once or twice and you're waiting and waiting and here comes ol' mama hen on the next ridge and, *yawk, yawk, yawk,* big boy's gone with her."

While Salter enjoys his reputation as a caller who fills the woods with turkey talk, he also knows the value of silence: "I've had the opportunity to hunt with a ton of people, and even experts call too much when the bird's already committed and coming in. Really, the best thing to do if you know a bird's on the way is to shut up. I may crank a turkey up and get him hammering, but when he's coming in, I'm gonna let him come in. If you keep calling he'll stop right there and gobble and gobble and gobble."

Hung-Up Turkeys

Gobblers hang up; that is, they stand there and gobble at you without coming into gun range, for all sorts of reasons. The main reason, of course, is that you, the hen, are supposed to go to them. Also, though turkeys can easily fly across rivers, ravines, fences, and just about anything else, they're notoriously reluctant to cross obstacles to get to a hen.

By calling to a hung-up gobbler, you encourage him to stay in one place, strutting and gobbling. Try shutting up and waiting him out. If you absolutely have to call while giving him the silent treatment, rake the leaves with your hand. Then you'll sound like a feeding hen who's nearby but ignoring the gobbler. It should drive him nuts.

Sometimes you have to move to fool a hung-up gobbler. When birds hang up on Ozarks guide Alex Rutledge, he'll back away from the turkey while calling, as if the hen is walking away. Then, Rutledge stops and sneaks back to his original position, raking leaves to simulate a feeding bird. If he's guiding a client, he'll pull the same trick by walking away calling, then finding a place to sit 100 yards behind his hunter. Thinking the hen is getting away, the gobbler will come closer, walking right past Rutledge's waiting client.

Salter likes to circle behind hung-up turkeys. "If I call and he interrupts my calls, but he doesn't come in, he's telling me he's a killable bird, but some element's bothering him, maybe a stream or a ditch that he doesn't want to cross," says Salter.

"I'll use a crow call to keep him gobbling and move around him, staying about 200 yards away. I like to get on the very back side of the bird because he's already traveled that route one time and he'll come back through there. Most of the time, if I can get all the way around a bird I can kill him."

WEATHER

When you wake to thunder rattling the windows or, worse, the howl of the wind whipping through the trees, fight the urge to bury your head in the pillow and close your eyes again.

Turkeys, after all, don't like bad weather any more than we do. But they cope with it and carry on with their lives. In fact, cold snaps and even heavy snowfalls don't seem to bother them in the least. On the other hand, a chilly wet dawn keeps turkeys on the roost longer and makes them gobble less. So does heavy fog.

Downpours drive turkeys to shelter, although they'll ignore gentler, all-day rains, often heading to open fields and gobbling well into the morning. In fact, one of the best mornings of hunting I ever had was a wet, drizzly morning in Missouri. Turkeys answered calls all morning long.

Poll any 10 experienced hunters, and every one of them will tell you they hate hunting in the wind most of all. When the wind blows, you can't hear the turkeys and they can't hear you. Unable to listen for danger, turkeys turn paranoid. Look for them in the fields or holed up in draws down out of the wind. Call loud and listen hard.

Back before I knew any better, I hunted in a spring storm when 45 m.p.h. winds drove the rain sideways in thick, stinging sheets. Gusts ripped heavy branches off trees, dropping them onto the ground with soggy, crashing thumps.

Through it all, I heard a bird gobbling, the sound snatched away by the wind almost before it registered as a turkey sound. That tom felt the urgency of the season, as if he knew spring is too short and unpredictable to wait for the perfect day. If turkeys can teach us a lesson in life, I believe that's it.

CHAPTER 7

Midday Turkeys

BY MY COUNT, Toby Bridges and I sat within earshot of a dozen gobblers at the edge of a burned field in northeast Missouri one clear, still morning last April. All around us, turkeys gobbled and clucked back and forth to one another, busily arranging rendezvous in the timber. When Bridges chipped in with some yelps of his own, two toms, invisible no more than 50 yards away in the brush behind us, gobbled back in unison. They answered every one of his calls eagerly, but in between gobbles we could hear the scolding yelps of an old hen who wouldn't let either bird leave her side. Bridges switched tactics and began trading insults with the hen, providing a whispered simultaneous translation from Turkey to English for my benefit. After an hour of heated bickering, the hen tired of the argument, turned snootily on her heel and lead both toms away, their gobbles eventually fading out in the distance. The woods grew quiet.

Left to my own devices, I would have done what many frustrated hunters do: declared the morning an exciting failure and gone home to bed. To quit early, I was about to learn in a most dramatic fashion, is to miss some of the best hunting of the day.

Bridges was far from discouraged. "In 30 years of hunting, I've probably called in more birds after 10:00 or 11:00 in the morning than I have at dawn," he told me as we left the field. "If we can find the right bird, he'll come running. What we do now is shop around 'til we find a hot turkey."

The hills of Putnam County aren't particularly steep, but there certainly are a lot of them. By lunchtime, Bridges had led me up one side and down the other of most of them twice, stopping every 150 yards or so to call.

Steve Pollick uses a box call to draw a gobble from an Ohio turkey. Walking and calling at midday can be an effective way to locate birds. *Photo by Julia C. McClellan.*

"Don't worry," he said confidently over his shoulder as he strode up yet another hill. "We'll pry a gobble out of a bird here yet."

Toiling up the slope behind him, I sneaked a look at my watch: 12:30, just half an hour before Missouri's 1:00 closing. I doubted we'd have time to set up on a bird and call it in even if Toby could make a bird gobble. Since my job on this hunt was to carry the gun and do what I was told, I kept my mouth shut and followed dutifully.

Bridges paused at the top of hill to yelp loudly on his box call and listen for an answer. "Lights are on, but nobody's home," he remarked, not for the first time on that long day. One hundred yards down the logging road, he purred and clucked softly on a mouth call. Immediately a loud gobble rattled back at us through the empty timber, its source no more than 70 yards away.

"That's a turkey!" I blurted involuntarily and altogether too loudly, sort of a human-shock gobble, and we scrambled to set up against the nearest tree.

Three soft yelps and 5 minutes later (including time spent shaking hands and slapping backs) I was, to my complete astonishment, fixing an out-of-state tag to the leg of a 24½-pound gobbler.

Welcome to midday turkey hunting.

WHY MIDDAY?

Gobbling, it's true, peaks during the first few hours of daylight. Early morning may be the easiest time to locate a bird and set up, but it can also be the hardest time of day to call a turkey into range. Most gobblers meet hens first thing in the morning at a predetermined spot. After flying down from the roost, toms may answer your calls excitedly while heading off in the opposite direction, urging you to follow along where their hens are waiting. Once a tom is actually with his harem, he has no reason to go look for another hen. In the natural scheme of turkey behavior hens go to the toms, not vice versa. The presence of other hunters in the woods early in the morning can also complicate our plans.

Later in the morning, however, hens wander off to sit on the nest, and gobblers find themselves at loose ends. From about 10:00 in the morning on, if you can locate these lonely toms you stand a good chance of calling them in. Moreover, you'll have very little competition from real hens or other hunters.

Don't give up at noon if your state allows afternoon hunting. Turkeys will gobble and come to a call all day long; shortly after our hunt, Bridges shot an Iowa gobbler at 4:00, using the same tactics he'd shown me.

MIDDAY TACTICS

Pro Mark Drury is another hunter who's tagged many birds between 10:00 A.M. and 1:00 P.M. Like Bridges, Drury swears by "running and

Author with a 24½-pound gobbler killed at midday.
Notice the high-noon shadows.

gunning" for turkeys. "I think it's just a case of covering the ground
and trying to up the odds," he says. "You're trying to find the right tom
in the right place. I think running and gunning works best later in the
spring, when the leaves are coming out and some of the hens are
done breeding, but I'd always rather keep moving and make something happen than sit and call blind." If you run and gun in crowded
woods, for safety's sake, wear blaze orange as you move through the
timber, making noises like a turkey.

How Drury hunts depends on the land. "If I've got a big national
forest to hunt," he says, "I like to cover as much ground as possible. If
I'm confined to a smaller area, I'll be more patient. There's a 200-acre
farm I hunt, near Warsaw, Missouri, where the fences have been bull-

dozed all along the perimeter. I'll walk the boundaries and stop and call for an hour in each of the four corners. That way I'm not just hunting that farm but calling to birds on adjacent properties. That 200 acres can make a good morning's hunt."

When he's moving at his preferred pace in the big woods, Drury stops to call for 5 minutes every 200 or 300 yards. On windy days, or any other time there's a lot of background noise (say, while hunting near a busy highway), Drury stops even more often, moving only 50 to 100 yards between calling sites. "When there's lots of background noise, a turkey that couldn't hear you when you called 50 yards back up the trail might hear you from your closer position," he notes.

I described my own hunt to Drury, telling him how Bridges's series of loud yelps 150 yards down the trail went unanswered but that a quiet cluck and purr brought an immediate response. "I've seen that happen many times," he said. "You know the turkey must hear you coming, but he doesn't answer until you're right on top of him. I think he hears the hen coming closer and closer and finally gobbles to say, "Here I am. Don't pass me by."

Some hunters work a variation on running and gunning by hunting their backtrails. By retracing their steps they hope to draw gobbles from birds that may have heard them calling as they walked through the woods earlier, and they don't want to let the "hen" get by them again.

Tony Knight of Modern Muzzleloading in Centerville, Iowa, has the most relaxed approach to midday hunting I've heard of. Knight hunts in the early morning, then returns to the shop on his farm at 8:00 or so and putters around. "A lot of times the turkeys will crank up again and gobble about 10:00 or 11:00. I keep my bibs and boots nearby like a fireman," he says. "When I hear them start gobbling again, I jump into my gear and go."

CALLING

As Mark Drury runs and guns through the woods, he begins with a crow call, then switches to soft yelps, increasing the volume if he gets no response. "I like to start with a crow call because I'd much rather strike a bird without sounding like another turkey. That way, I can take a little more time to set up without bumping a bird that's looking for me." While some hunters prefer to start out with a loud, aggressive call, hoping to shock a bird into gobbling, Drury likens calling to climbing a ladder. "Start at the bottom and go up [in volume] rung by rung. It's hard to go back down if you start out too loud, but you can always make the next call a little louder."

Cutting is a popular call for many hunters trying to provoke a gobble, but both Drury and Bridges stick primarily with yelps. Says Drury, "I'd say 90 percent of the turkeys I call in come to a series of yelps. That's the backbone of turkey calling. If my yelping hasn't brought a response I'll sometimes mix in some cutting at the end."

Bridges agrees with Drury: "A lot of hunters want to master all the sounds of the wild turkey and wind up not making any of them really well," he says. "Me, I'd rather be the best yelper in the woods. I do like to mix in some purrs and clucks, because I think that's more natural; hens don't just yelp all the time, and I think a tom knows there's something wrong if he doesn't hear some clucking and purring in between the loud yelps."

WHEN TO LEAVE THEM

When they're using run-and-gun tactics, both Bridges and Drury will give up quickly on birds they deem unenthusiastic. "I call that first gobble from a bird a 'courtesy gobble,'" says Drury, "If he answers just once and doesn't make any sign of coming closer in 10 or 15 minutes, that's a sure indication to me that he's with hens and won't be coming at all. Then I'll leave him and look for another bird. Of course, if I'm hunting a small area and I can't pick and choose my turkeys, I'll be more patient with any bird I get to gobble, even if he doesn't come in right away."

On another midday hunt with Bridges, we struck a bird on our very first call. Bridges couldn't make the turkey gobble again, so we shrugged and set off on our way. An hour and a half later, we'd made a big loop and were coming back to the spot where we'd first heard the gobbler answer. And there he was, standing on the logging road, still looking for the "hen" he'd heard earlier. If we'd sat down when we first heard the gobble and waited that turkey out, we might have eventually killed him.

Alex Rutledge examines fresh tracks. Sometimes setting up near fresh sign and blind calling works well at midday, especially near open fields.

Some hunters prefer to sit for long periods in good habitat in the middle of the day. They point out that most of the turkeys they kill come in silently. A run-and-gun type of hunter will walk right past any number of silent but callable turkeys and never even know they're there. Perhaps the most pleasant way to hunt turkeys is to combine the two methods; walk and call until you find a place to sit and call quietly for 45 minutes or so.

Which method works best? My theory is this: In areas with high turkey densities, sitting still might be more effective. There are so many turkeys that gobblers don't have to run all over the woods looking for hens. By the same token, running and gunning might work better in areas where turkeys aren't as plentiful and where toms will travel a long way to meet a lonely hen. How you hunt depends on your own preferences, too. If you hate sitting still, walk. If patience is your strength, sit.

"I might get a little antsy sometimes and leave a bird too soon," Bridges admitted to me, "but running and gunning is a system that works for me. If I leave a bird I'll remember where he is and come back to him an hour or so later. Sometimes the commotion of calling to a bird with hens sets the stage for later on in the day. He'll remember the "hen" he heard earlier and come looking for her once his own hens have left him."

Ponder that for a moment. How many times have you unknowingly made a date with a tom for later in the morning, then stood him up by going home to bed? Imagine him out there, mooning around the woods, gobbling his head off forlornly, looking for you. That's a thought to keep you out in the timber long after dawn, isn't it?

CHAPTER

Low-Impact Turkey Hunting

L isten to the run-and-gun hunters who tear up the woods in search of that one hot turkey, and they'll tell you that a turkey hunter needs hundreds, even thousands, of acres to roam.

The old-time turkey hunters did it differently. They built a blind, sat down to a turkey, and patiently called to him. If they didn't kill the gobbler one morning, they'd come back the next and try him again. The old-school style of turkey hunting strikes many of us as stodgy, boring, even a little quaint.

Walter Parrot knows better. Winner of sixteen world and national turkey calling titles, Parrot grew up hunting small woodlots around Fredericktown, in southeast Missouri. He knows that 20 or 30 acres can be all the room a patient hunter needs to tag a turkey. Give Parrot two or three 40-acre woodlots, and he's set for the whole season. Since many of us don't have the luxury of hunting huge tracts of private land, Parrot's advice on hunting small woods is worth heeding.

"Hunting little 20- or 40-acre woodlots, I learned you can spend a whole season hunting one bird in a small area if you're careful not to spook him," says Parrot. "And if you've got permission to hunt 40 acres next to land where no hunting is allowed, you've got a real honeyhole. If you can find two or three small areas that turkeys use regularly, you've got all the hunting land you need right there."

One bird in particular taught Parrot several valuable lessons about hunting small woods. "I'd taken a few birds, but this was my first tough turkey," he says. "It lived on 42 acres. My cousin lived across the road from that bird, and he'd hunt him every morning before work. He kept me up on what that turkey was doing."

Walt Parrot took this bird from a small woodlot. The key, says Parrot, is to be patient, and to
be extra careful not to spook any birds.

One day, after his cousin left the woods for work, Parrot tried hunting the turkey himself. "My Uncle had told me that late morning hunts
were often productive, and my cousin had shown me the route he'd
been taking into the bird every morning. I slipped in the same way at
10:00 A.M., and killed the turkey at 12:45 by playing hard to get.

"I learned three important lessons from that bird: You can hunt
the same turkey day after day; turkeys will respond to a call that
sounds different from what they've been hearing; and, if you have the
patience to stay with a bird, you can kill it."

Small-woods hunting is a study in finesse. "You don't want to run
that turkey off or your hunt is over for the morning," says Parrot. With
that thought in mind, you need to scout the woods well before the
season begins. "Learn where all the fences and creeks are, and how to
get in and out of the woods without being seen," Parrot advises. "Be
careful in your scouting. You don't want to run into the gobbler until
you're ready to hunt."

Once the season starts, always err on the side of caution. "In the morning, set up 150 yards or more away from him. You can always move closer, but if you bust him off the roost the hunt is over for the day."

Parrot also believes you should take your time and choose your calling site very carefully. "Too many hunters hear a bird gobble and then sit down at the first tree nearby. Don't be in such a hurry. You know where that turkey is and he's not going anywhere. Remember, you're in his living room and he knows when anything's out of place. Don't skyline yourself. Pick a good spot."

Choose a tree that's wider than your shoulders, both for safety's sake and to break up your outline. Try to find a place where you'll be in the shade for at least the next two hours. Parrot carries a pair of pruning clippers and clears himself a place to sit and swing his shotgun. "Don't throw the brush away after you cut it," he says. "Stick it in the ground in front of you to help break up your outline. With the camo we have today (Parrot wears Mossy Oak), it doesn't take very much brush to make it harder for the turkey to see you."

Where you sit matters, too. "Some hunters like to sit close to the crest of a hill so they can't see the bird—and it can't see them—until it's within gun range. I disagree. What if a different bird comes in silently from an unexpected direction, or your turkey shuts up and circles around you? I'd rather back off a little way so that if I have to move I have time to let the turkey get behind a tree before he's too close. Ideally, I'd like to shoot him at about thirty yards. That's close enough to be sure, but far enough away for my pattern to open up a little to make up for any mistakes I make pointing the gun."

Wherever you set up, be sure it's a place where you can comfortably spend a long time waiting. Parrot learned early that his chances for success climbed if he was willing to stay with a turkey.

"He may be with hens, but if you're persistent, sooner or later he might come over," says Parrot. "I don't care how good a caller you are, if a tom's with hens, 95 percent of the time you can't do anything with him."

Parrot beats henned-up toms with patience. "I've sat and called to a turkey for more than two hours, clucking softly and scratching the leaves to sound like a feeding hen. Then, when the bird finally gobbles, I'll just give a few yelps every once in a while. A lot of times, playing hard to get will aggravate him so much that he'll come in."

Despite all the calling titles he's won, Parrot calls sparingly in the woods: "I don't call aggressively unless I have to. You can always add more calling, but you can't take it away. I believe a lot of people hang turkeys up by calling too much."

Parrot uses Knight and Hale calls, and takes several into the woods. "I like to use two calls—usually a mouth call and box—to sound like two different hens. Also, if the turkey sees me, I'll change to a different call."

One morning often isn't enough to wear down a gobbler. Parrot believes you can go to the same spot and call to the same bird morning after morning. "Every day that turkey wakes up in a different frame of mind. He keeps hearing that same hen in the same place. Eventually, he'll get tired of his hens and want to see this new hen he's been hearing," Parrot says. "You can tell when a gobbler's tired of his hens when he leads them to you."

You might have to spend one day with a bird, or five days. "It varies," says Parrot. "A buddy of mine hunted the same bird all season. He finally got one chance and messed it up.

"Each morning, you want to slip in and keep probing. If he flies down and goes in the opposite direction one morning, then you want to set up on the other side of the roost the next morning. If he gobbles but doesn't come, stay where you are and be patient."

Another tactic for a tough bird is to hunt someplace else first thing in the morning, then try him around 10:00 or 11:00 A.M. instead. Parrot takes great pains to ease into the woods undetected when he does a late-morning hunt. "I don't like to make turkey sounds when I'm moving into the woods; a turkey can come to you before you're ready. Instead, I ease slowly into the woods, staying as quiet as possible. I almost still-hunt my way in. I'll stop to use a crow or hawk call to try to make him gobble, and I always pay attention to the woods around me. A turkey might not sound off, but you may see bluejays flying low to harass him, or hear squirrels chattering at a turkey in strut."

Even if you never hear the bird, you know he's there somewhere. "That's one of the big advantages of hunting a small piece of property," says Parrot. "It's not like hunting a 50,000-acre tract of timber when you don't even know if birds are there. You know the turkey is there on your little parcel whether he gobbles or not. And that keeps your confidence level high."

Parrot has hunted more than his share of rainy mornings when the birds were quiet. As a bricklayer, he can't work in the rain, so

When Parrot is facing a tough turkey, he'll often switch his tactics and hunt in the late morning. He'll try to get a bird to shockgobble as he goes into the woods; otherwise, he'll try to remain as silent as possible.

those are the days he gets to hunt. "It doesn't bother me when the birds don't gobble, because I know where they are."

BLIND LUCK

Last spring I hunted with turkey expert Ray Eye, at his camp in northern Missouri. Eye leases 4,600 acres of pasture and woods in the best turkey country in the U.S. His place is dotted with 30 turkey blinds, a few in the woods, most of them along field edges.

"When we first got this property, we were still running and gunning. We figured it was just big enough for a couple of people to hunt at one time," says Eye. Then Eye set up all of his blinds. That first spring, he hosted ten hunters on opening day. Eight tagged birds in the season's first hour; the other two killed turkeys the next morning.

Camouflage blinds help prevent birds from becoming people shy.

Eye scouts throughout the winter and early spring, setting up blinds near fields or openings where birds come to strut. The blind may be near a turkey roost or several hundred yards from where the birds spend the night. Hunters sneak into the blinds before daylight. Eye instructs them to cluck and yelp softly and, if nothing happens, to sneak out when the hunt is over.

Accustomed to tiptoeing through the woods to set up on gobbling turkeys before dawn, and running and gunning later in the day, I had my reservations about hunting from a blind. Too confining, too boring. I thought that if you have to hunt turkeys this way, you may as well just hunt whitetails instead. The design of Eye's blinds underscored my sentiment. He'd taken swivel seats and shooting rails from treestands, set them on the ground, then surrounded them with camo burlap. Small shooting windows were cut out of the burlap.

I soon found that hunting from a blind has its own charms. The first morning I called up two hens, who spent two hours scratching and clucking within 25 yards of me. Invisible in the blind, I could stretch, fidget, fiddle with calls, eat a granola bar, drink coffee and generally enjoy a delightful morning, occasionally peering out the window to see if a gobbler had joined my hens. None ever did. Eventually, in the spirit of Eye's low-impact methods, I snuck out the back door and crawled off through the woods to keep from spooking the hens away.

"Hunting from blinds may not be as much fun as running and gunning and trying to make something happen," says Eye, "but most people are interested in the end result, which is a dead bird. On this property at least, we've found hunting from a blind is the best way to kill a turkey."

Eye's lease is wide-open country, even by north Missouri standards. Spend much time walking through the pastures and small woodlots, and you'll see turkeys several hundreds away that have already spotted you and are running away. The openness of the landscape and the high densities of turkeys in Eye's area make it a natural for blind hunting, but the technique will work almost anywhere, so long as you scout your area carefully.

Another benefit to hunting from blinds is that it confines hunters, and prevents them from moving around and disturbing the birds. "Turkeys don't get call shy," he says. "They get people shy. Now that we've gone to the blinds we have gobbling turkeys on this place all season long. The people next to us complain that their turkeys quit gobbling three days into the season. That's because they're moving through the woods scaring turkeys."

Tough Turkeys

The tradition of the "tough turkey"—the wise old bird that everyone hunts and no one can kill—lives on throughout the country. Usually the bird wears a nickname and the scalps of a long string of frustrated hunters as the season wears on. Any visiting hunter with a reputation as an expert is assigned the tough turkey, whether he wants him or not.

Call maker Will Primos draws his share of tough turkeys on his travels. His first reaction to a tough turkey is the same as yours or mine: "I say, no, I don't want him. Give me one of those young dumb two-year olds instead."

In all seriousness, Primos has learned that tough turkeys often aren't as tough as their reputations. As the tough turkey's legend grows, hunters forget that turkeys are essentially creatures of habit, and that in the woods, hens go to the toms, not vice versa. "People give hard-to-kill turkeys human attributes, they say they're tough or smart or whatever," says Primos. "A lot of times, those turkeys aren't so hard to kill. They walk away from hunters gobbling not because they're super-smart or wary, but because they know where they're going and they want the hen to come with them."

Moreover, hunters fall into a rut of approaching tough turkeys the same way every time, all season long, hoping their calling skill alone can help them succeed where others have failed.

"They're not going to come running in just because you're a good caller," Primos advises. "You've got to wait them out." Patience is the hunter's best weapon against a tough turkey. Often, a bird that walks away from a hunter gobbling will come back later in the morning after his hens have left him. "Give them time. Blind up and sit tight. Scratch the leaves and cluck softly," advises Primos. He recalls a hunt

Will Primos circled around and came in from a
side that this gobbler wasn't paying attention to.
Approach is critical, says Primos.

several years ago in Georgia with his friend Ron Petty, where
patience almost killed a tough old gobbler.

"We set up on the same ridge as a roosted tom," says Primos. "I
always like to be on the west side of a turkey because I believe they
instinctively don't like to walk into the morning sun. It distorts their
vision and makes it harder for them to see predators. So we set up to
the west, and of course the turkey went east, gobbling."

Below the ridgetop, Primos spotted a logged, three-acre clearing.
"I suggested to Ron that we go down to the clearing, take a nap, then
wake up and call every once in while. I figured the bird would come
back sooner or later."

After alternately dozing and calling for a couple of hours, Primos
woke up, slipped a call into his mouth, and heard the drumming of a
turkey nearby before he could even cluck. "He was within 20 yards. A
lot of times, turkeys will drum instead of gobbling as they come

through the woods, so they won't let other critters know where they are. You have to listen for that sound."

Although Primos could hear the bird, he couldn't see it or pinpoint its location. "Sometimes that drumming sound just kind of surrounds you and you can't tell where it's coming from. The turkey got within five yards of us," he remembers. "Ron couldn't reach his gun, and I couldn't reach mine, but his was beside me. I picked it up and tried to shoot the bird, but his gun's safety is in a different place than mine. By the time I figured it out and got the safety off, the turkey saw us, took off, and I missed."

Lousy Clucks and Purrs

What call do you make to the turkey who's heard it all, who's listened to every cutt, cluck, yelp and whine in the woods?

Again, the problem is usually not that the turkey has become call-shy, but that he expects any hen that calls to him to come running.

"My favorite 'call' makes lousy clucks and purrs," Primos says of the turkey wing. In fact, he's used a wing cut from a hen turkey for years as an ace in the hole for tough gobblers. Primos began marketing a version of his secret weapon this spring, calling it "The Real Wing."

Primos recalls a particularly tough turkey he hunted with his wing. "Everyone had been hunting this bird. He'd gobble, then walk away. They called him Old Mossy, because he lived on a moss hill. I got assigned to hunt him one morning even though I didn't want him."

When they dumped him out of the truck that morning, Primos didn't try to hoot or crow call. Instead, as he walked toward the turkey's roost, he made sure to rustle the leaves as a feeding hen would. ("A turkey's got two feet just like you," Primos explains. "All you have to do to sound like a hen is take two steps, then sweep one foot to the side like you're scratching for acorns.")

"Old Mossy gobbled when he heard me walk," Primos continues. "I got below the ridge, sat down, then scratched lightly and purred."

The turkey flew down 150 yards from Primos' stand. Instead of calling, Primos took the turkey wing from his vest and flapped it lightly, like a hen stretching her wings. The thought of a closeby hen not responding to his gobbles was too much for the gobbler to take.

"He was so frustrated that he flew up into a tree at the ridgetop to look for the hen. He gobbled three times, hopped off the branch, ran into range, and I killed him," Primos remembers.

Primos' turkey wing works for many reasons, not the least of which is that turkeys haven't heard nearly as much flapping as they have cutting and yelping during the season. Even more important, flapping or scratching leaves tells a gobbler there's a hen nearby that's not responding to his calls. Again, we're tempted to assign a human personality to the turkey, and believe that his vanity is wounded if he knows there's hen nearby who won't come to him. Primos has a more logical explanation: "If gobbling isn't attracting the hen, he goes to his second tactic. Gobbling is the first tactic, being seen is the second."

LOUIS

Another reason turkeys earn reputations as being tough is that no one thinks to hunt them in a different way. Tough turkeys often face a steady stream of hunters coming at them during the course of the season. All too often, the hunters fall into the rut of approaching from the same direction, and setting up in the same place. Don't be afraid to try something different on a bird no one can call. Over the years, Primos has killed his share of tough gobblers simply by taking another route into the woods. A perfect example is the bird he named "Louis."

"I named him Louis because he lived behind the house of a man named Louis, who was caretaker of the property," recalls Primos. "No one could kill this turkey. People would leave from the house and cross the pasture and try to hunt him. Louis had a horse and mule in the back, and when you crossed the pasture they'd stare at you. That turkey would see them staring and quit gobbling. The gobbler watched that horse and mule to warn him of trouble."

One morning Primos took a wide detour, avoiding the pasture entirely and coming in to set up behind Louis. "I got in long before daylight and set up within 50 yards of his tree. I never even called, but when he flew down, he landed in range and I shot him."

Strange, perhaps, for a callmaker to admit to killing a turkey without ever touching a call, but Will Primos knows that taking the tough turkeys sometimes means doing things no one else would think of.

CHAPTER 10

Hunting with Decoys

THE TWO GOBBLERS in the cornfield strutted uneasily, their attention divided between the Outlaw hen silhouettes at the field's edge and the two bark-colored lumps sitting at the base of a skinny oak. One of the lumps balanced an 1100 on one knee. The other sat plugging its fingers into its ears, anticipating the shotgun's report.

"They don't like this," whispered my partner. "They know something's wrong."

"What is it?" I whispered back, unplugging my ears.

"They don't like *us,*" he said, steadying his aim as the birds swung their eyes our way. The gobblers wavered indecisively, torn between survival and mating instinct. The gun boomed, one bird went down and the second scrambled for safety.

Sometimes decoys bring dramatic results; turkeys have been known to attack jake decoys and try to breed plastic hens. On other occasions, as in that Illinois cornfield, a decoy may just tip the balance in your favor, allaying a bird's suspicions for just a second too long. In fact, the effect of a decoy on a gobbler might be no more than a subtle distraction that allows you to cock a hammer or shift your gun barrel undetected when the turkey is in close.

Hunters have used decoys since long before Columbus; Albert Hazen Wright in *Early Records of the Wild Turkey* (1914), quoted a nineteenth-century account of a traditional Cherokee hunting method not that different from our own: "Having prepared from the skin an apt resemblance of the living bird, they follow the turkey trails or haunts till they discover a flock, when they secrete themselves behind a log in such a manner to elude discovery, partially displaying their decoy and imitating the gobbling noise of the cock."

80

Matt Morrett sets up a hen decoy. *Photo by Julia C. McClellan.*

In modern times, however, decoys have only recently gained widespread acceptance. Until the development of the collapsible foam-type decoys made by Featherflex, Delta, Flambeau, and others, as well as the equally portable Outlaw silhouettes, few hunters wanted to carry full-body turkey decoys with them into the woods. Now, anyone can carry a flock of decoys with them.

Decoys are a valuable addition to your hunting arsenal, but a decoy is no substitute for bad calling, inadequate scouting, or being in the wrong place at the wrong time. You can't just stick a decoy in the ground and hope for a turkey to walk by. Some days, decoys don't work at all, and they can even cause a bird to hang up. Don't become overdependent on decoys; people have killed lots of turkeys without them. Sometimes setting out decoys isn't worth the risk of spooking a gobbler if he's nearby.

Multiple-decoy sets have become popular with many hunters. Adding a jake to this flock of Outlaw hens drew this Merriam's gobbler looking for a fight. *Photo courtesy Outlaw Decoys.*

That said, a decoy in the right place can work wonders. It can literally bring a turkey running. Here are some tips for decoy use.

DECOY HOW-TO

- Set decoys about 20 yards in front of you. If a gobbler hangs up outside the decoys, he may still be in gun range.
- One hen decoy is good, two or three hens are better.
- Motion adds tremendous realism to decoys. Set a collapsible

foam decoy on a piece of aluminum arrow shaft, and it will move back and forth in the lightest breeze.

• Field edges are a prime location to set decoys later in the morning. Set out your decoys, build a blind and "blind-call," that is, call softly every 15 minutes whether you see something or not. It's a dull way to hunt, but if you're patient, it will work.

• If you're trying to hunt a gobbler that struts in the middle of a field, find out where he enters and leaves the field and set your decoys there, in gun range of your hiding place at the field's edge.

• Hen decoys are most effective late in the season, when the majority of hens are on the nest.

• Hen decoys are least effective when gobblers are accompanied by lots of hens.

• Jake decoys work best early in the season, when gobblers are still traveling together. Use slow, drawn-out gobbler yelps with a jake decoy.

• Where afternoon hunting is legal, many hunters like to set out a flock of decoys where a tom will pass by them on his way to the roost.

• Fall hunters, when they break up a flock, should set one or two decoys out at the scatter point.

• A flock of 6 to 10 decoys can be very effective in the fall. Scout until you know where birds are roosting and feeding. The very best spot for a decoy flock is near a roost in the morning, along the bird's route of travel to a feeding area. Build a blind nearby and aggressively mimic the calls the real turkeys are making.

• To keep gobblers from hanging up and displaying at long distance, try to set your decoy where a bird won't see it until he's in gun range, say, around a bend in a field or behind a small rise. For safety's sake, you need to be able to see beyond the decoy, however.

• A scattered flock of 6 to 10 decoys can work well if you hunt from a blind in the spring. Spread them out in front of your blind so they'll attract birds into shooting lanes to the left, right, and in front.

• Some hunters believe a gobbler will display to a decoy's face.

They set their decoys facing their hide, so the bird will come around between the hunter and the decoy for a close shot.

THE BREEDING-HEN SET

The latest trick among decoy users is to make a "breeding hen" by shortening the decoy's stake so you can easily set her with her belly touching the ground. That's the posture a hen assumes when she's ready to be bred.

A breeding hen by herself may lure in a gobbler, but if you add a jake right behind her, as if he's about to breed the hen, it should drive the tom nuts, especially early in the season.

Turkeys have a rigid flock pecking order, and no adult male turkey will tolerate the sight of a jake breeding a hen.

Hunters like me, who don't mind shooting jakes, add a second hen, 5 yards farther away and off to the side. The theory here is that a real jake will shy away from fighting the jake decoy, and he'll go to the single hen decoy instead.

If you use this set, make sure you have a clear field of fire at the jake and second hen decoy.

DECOY SAFETY

- Turkey hunters always have to be careful in the woods. Obviously, using decoys—especially jakes—means you have to raise your safety precautions to a new level.

- Don't hide too well; sit against a tree or a rock that's wider than your shoulders and tall enough to protect the back of your head in case someone comes up from behind and takes a shot at your decoy.

- The greatest danger in decoy hunting comes when another hunter stalks the decoy from the opposite side, putting you in his line of fire. From your seated position identify the clearest line of vision to your front. Establish a sight line that allows you 100 yards of visibility. Then set your decoy(s) approximately 20 yards from your position on the line.

- If another hunter does stalk your decoys, don't wave your hand. Don't move, just speak out in a loud, clear voice.

- If you are calling over decoys and elect to move to a new stand, check carefully that no one is stalking your decoys. Check before leaving your stand tree. Should you see someone in the area, the preceding rule applies.

- Wear gloves and a face mask. In the excitement of the hunt, white hands or a sunburned face can look just like a turkey's head.

- When you walk through the woods, carry your decoys hidden in a pack or in the gamebag of your vest.

Modern decoys, whether foam or silhouette, are so light you can pack a whole flock easily. Last spring I hunted three states with a sack of Outlaws on my back; I forgot they were there until I needed them. Oh, and by the way, after one too many early-morning wake-ups, a packsack full of silhouettes makes a nice backrest when you lean against the sharp bark of a tree to nod off in the woods.

11

Turkey-Hunting Safety

L AST SPRING, my friend Steve stepped into a clearing to see his hunting partner studying him through the crosshairs of a shotgun scope. "He was only 40 yards away. I couldn't believe he thought I was a turkey," says Steve, "so I waved to him."

Steve's partner shot him in the face.

Doctors were able to remove one of the two pellets that hit Steve. He'll carry the other embedded in his cheekbone for the rest of his life. Getting shot in the face ruined Steve's enthusiasm for turkey hunting. He plans to fish in the spring from now on.

Steve looks nothing like a turkey; neither do any of the rest of us. Turkey hunting, nevertheless, owns a near-monopoly on "victim mistaken for game" accidents.

THE TRUTH ABOUT TURKEY-HUNTING SAFETY

Several truths about turkey-hunting safety might surprise you. The hunters most likely to be involved in accidents aren't rookies; instead, they're usually veterans of 20 seasons or more. In fact, despite the numbers of new hunters coming to the sport, accidents have fallen by nearly 50 percent since 1992, thanks to safety programs conducted by the National Wild Turkey Federation, hunter education instructors, and others. In the spring of 1998, turkey hunters across the nation were killed or injured at a rate of just 4.64 hunters per 100,000 participants. Compare that injury rate to swimming or boating, and you'll see turkey hunting is actually quite safe.

Safety should always be uppermost in every turkey hunter's mind. Several states issue safety stickers with every turkey license.

In fact, turkey-hunting accidents actually occur at a lower rate than all hunting accidents. Perhaps the perception of turkey hunting as extremely dangerous encourages hunters, especially neophytes, to be extra careful.

Rifles, legal for turkey hunting in only six states, are nonetheless involved in a high percentage of fatal accidents. Rifles accounted for just 10 percent of overall accidental shootings in the turkey woods recorded between 1985 and 1992. However, 24 of the 97 rifle shootings were fatal. Shotguns, on the other hand, were used in 879 shootings, with only 22 fatalities resulting.

Fluorescent orange, now required in Pennsylvania during the fall season and for hunters walking through the woods in the spring, hasn't yet proved conclusively to reduce accident rates. Accident rates dropped initially when Pennsylvania mandated orange, then rebounded 2 years after the law went into effect. Moreover, small patches of hunter orange have even been identified as a factor in some accidents. Even worse, faded orange often appears red in the woods; the same color as a turkey's head.

Steve Puppe and Julia McClellan pack a gobbler into a fluorescent-orange bag for safe transport on public land. *Photo by Julia C. McClellan.*

MISTAKEN FOR GAME

Regardless of whether hunters use rifles or wear orange, there would be no accidental shootings if hunters identified their targets properly.

Turkey hunters wear full camo and make noises like turkeys. Even so, it's baffling to anyone that hunters can mistake people for turkeys. The psychological phenomenon called "premature closure" explains how otherwise rational people can look at a hunter and see a turkey. Essentially, you see one or two clues or visual indicators of what you're looking for—say, a flash of red, white, or blue—and your mind jumps ahead, filling in the rest of the details until it sees what it wants to see—a turkey.

You might scoff. I did too, until I mistook a person for a turkey two years ago. Four of us were hunting together on a farm in Illinois. We'd split up into pairs, and Ray Eye and I had both tagged our birds by 6:30 in the morning. We left our turkeys and guns and went looking for Peter and Mike, the other two hunters in our party.

As we walked down a trail in the open timber, I saw a red head bobbing toward us, 40 yards away, "That's a turkey!" I said over my shoulder to Ray, then turned back and was stunned to see that the "turkey" was actually Mike walking up the trail in plain sight. The red turkey head was his farmer's face, burned by the sun. Mike's camo clothes had blended into the background, leaving only that red face visible, and my mind made up the rest. That, I realized soberly, is how people get shot.

Premature closure can happen to anyone at any time, but surprisingly, veteran hunters are more likely to make mistakes. Beginners aren't as keyed in to the visual clues of a turkey; they often don't know they're seeing a turkey until they've seen the whole bird. Moreover, we've done such a good job of educating new hunters to the dangers of the turkey woods that most novices hunt in a state of barely controlled terror.

Experienced hunters see a glimpse of red, say, and their mind can fill in the blanks. Moreover, veteran hunters often have reputations to maintain. Peer pressure to tag a turkey adds stresses that can lead to accidents in the woods.

Still, there's a simple cure for premature closure; don't shoot until you've seen a whole turkey and a beard. Condition yourself only to shoot at birds within a range of 35 yards; most "mistaken for game" shootings occur at 35 yards or more (despite what you hear about new turkey chokes and loads, 20 to 35 yards remains the optimum turkey-killing distance anyway).

RULES TO LIVE BY

The National Wild Turkey Federation has made several studies of turkey-hunting accidents. Most occur early in the morning, when

Pick a tree wider than your shoulders to protect your back. *Photo by Julia C. McClellan.*

hunters expect to see turkeys and visibility is poor. Hunters in full camo are least likely to be mistaken for turkeys. It's those people whose incomplete camo reveals a shock of white hair, say, or a red bandana who are at much greater risk. Always call out to another hunter in a loud, clear voice. Steve's partner thought he saw a turkey. When Steve waved, the motion convinced him.

Here are the NWTF's safety guidelines:

1. Never wear pieces of clothing that contain the colors red, white, or blue, because they can be mistaken for colors found on wild turkeys.
2. Be sure that the accessories you carry that are red, white, and blue (e.g., diaphragm calls, box-call chalk, candy wrappers, apples, cigarette packs, etc.) are not visible to other hunters.
3. Camouflage your gun. If you don't, at least cover up white diamonds or other red or white markings.
4. Always keep your hands and head camouflaged when calling.

5. Wear dark-colored socks and pants that are long enough to keep your bare skin from being exposed.
6. Do not overcamouflage yourself by sitting in vegetation so thick that it obscures your vision.
7. If you can legally use a manmade blind of camouflage netting, maintain a clear field of view.

There's another adjustment you can make: to your attitude. Hunters who put pressure on themselves to kill a bird make dangerous mistakes. Relax, enjoy the woods, the season, the country, and the people you hunt with. You don't have to kill a turkey to have a successful season. Certainly, you won't starve if the turkey gets away, nor will the bird return to carry off your children in revenge. The worst thing that happens is that the gobbler gets to live for another year. And there's nothing really the matter with that.

12

CHAPTER

Boats and Bikes

W ILD TURKEYS and bassboats might, at first glance, seem to have as much in common as, well, largemouth bass and box calls. Yet on many big impoundments, you're simply not dressed for spring unless you fish in full camo.

"What a lot of us on Bull Shoals Lake will do is fish from midnight to dawn, then start turkey hunting from the boat at gobbling time," says Dody Rorie, a die-hard turkey hunter who works for Ranger Boats in Flippin, Arkansas. "We even have people fish bass tournaments on Bull Shoals in their hunting clothes. These guys will bail out of a tournament in a minute if they hear a turkey."

It's anyone's guess how many thousands or millions of acres of prime turkey woods lie within the boundaries of U.S. Army Corps, power-company, and TVA lakes nationwide, but much of that land is wide open to the public. To hunt reservoir turkeys most effectively, though, you need a boat.

The impoundment turkey hunter confronts the same dilemma as the bass angler on a big lake: an almost overwhelming amount of likely habitat to search. Bull Shoals, for instance, sprawls into two states, boasting literally hundreds of miles of timbered, zigzagging shoreline. Waterborne turkey hunters meet the challenge of big reservoirs by prospecting, the same way bass fishermen do on a new lake. Hunters move quickly from cove to cove using an attractor—a box call, a hoot, a caw—loud and brassy, like a fast-moving buzzbait, hoping to "strike" a bird. The boat that's evolved to cover miles of bass water makes perfect sense for reservoir turkey hunters.

"You can work far more country in a boat at prime gobbling time, from dawn to 8:30 or 9:00, than you ever could on foot," says Rorie,

A bassboat allows you to cover plenty of ground while searching for turkeys and to sneak in a little fishing as well.

explaining his methods: "I'll run into the back of a cove, and owl-call or crow-call or cutt, or maybe I'll blow one of those silent dog whistles. It's much easier to hear a bird when you're on the water; with those ridges on either side of the cove, it's like he's gobbling inside a tunnel."

There's no particular need to use a trolling motor or muffle the oarlocks when you're on the water, either, according to Rorie. "Our turkeys get hunted hard from land and water, and they're wary, but they hear boats from the day they're hatched. I really don't think the motor bothers them," explains Rorie. "I used to try to be real sneaky when I'd strike a bird and switch to the trolling motor. I finally realized I could crank up the outboard, get there quicker, and not spook the bird. I've got a 200-horse Yamaha on my boat, and if anything

Toby Bridges hits the beach after striking an Iowa gobbler.

scares turkeys, that would," he says, laughing. "Sometimes, if you start up the engine and shut it off, you'll even make a bird gobble."

Once a bird gobbles, Rorie heads up into the cove until he's behind the turkey, then beaches the boat and slips up into the woods, trying to circle around above him. With water on three sides of him, the bird is likely to head uphill toward what Rorie calls "the mainland." "When you can set up where that bird wants to go, it triples your chances of calling him in," Rorie concludes.

Although many hunters go back to fishing after 9:00 A.M., Rorie considers the middle of the day prime time to hunt from a boat. Once the hens leave the gobblers to sit on their nests, the lonely toms wander the timber, looking for company. Cover enough water, and sooner or later you'll find a lonely bird that will answer your call eagerly. In the evening, the boat makes an excellent listening platform for roosting birds.

Author and Randy McPherren admire an Iowa gobbler.

Turkeys often relate to the structure created by flooding a riverbed the same way that bass relate to features below a lake's surface. Take Truman Lake, in Missouri. "When they flooded the lake, the hollows filled up, leaving the ridges above water," one Missouri hunter told me. "There's a stretch of old backcountry gravel road across every one of those ridges. You might have half a mile of flat road between coves, and the gobblers love to strut back and forth on them. When it's wet, they don't like to get their feathers soaked, and then they really hit those old roads. When the water level's down, you'll spot birds strutting along the bare shore, too."

Consult a topo map of the reservoir as you plan your hunt. Look for flats along ridges, old roads, clearings, or any other place a bird might strut.

Often, a boat is virtually the only way to reach public land on reservoirs and impoundments. In many cases, the public land bordering reservoirs is itself surrounded by private ground, leaving the public effectively cut off from their own property. Once, back when I still thought of turkey hunting as a purely terrestrial pursuit, I finagled permission to cross a large chunk of private ground to reach the U.S. Army Corps of Engineers land on my local reservoir. I parked the car long before dawn and hiked up and down ridges, tore through briars, tripped over fences, walked into branches, and generally staggered about, only to be greeted by the unwelcome call of "Hunter over here!" when I reached my destination. I felt the way mountaineers must when they reach a summit only to find someone else's flag.

The other hunter's secret? The glittering bassboat beached in the cove, of course, a sight as astonishing to me back then as if he'd moored a flying saucer to a tree. Neither of us shot a bird that morning, but I was the one with the long walk home.

Boating for gobblers isn't just confined to reservoirs. Turkeys live along rivers and streams, too, and a boat can take you deep into state and national forests where hunters rarely venture on foot. "I've floated the Buffalo River many times," says Rorie, "just drifting with the motor off. It's certainly the most pleasant way to hunt turkeys there is. If you have enough water to turn around and run back upstream, river hunting can work very well."

River hunting does have its drawbacks. "In a river," explain Rorie, "you're way down in the bottoms and the ridgetops are high up, while in a reservoir, you're much closer to the ridgetops and you can hear the birds better. Also, if you're on a river and a turkey gobbles on up a feeder creek, you won't hear him unless you happen to be floating right by the mouth at the time."

Bear in mind, too, that although most navigable rivers are open to the public, the shoreline may be privately owned; if you choose to float a river for turkeys, be sure you're hunting public land or have permission to hunt private ground. In some cases, islands belong to the public. There's a small group of hunters around my area who boat out to the wooded islands on the Mississippi where turkeys rarely see a hunter.

Biking for Turkeys

John Miller, a turkey-hunting fanatic from Ridgefield, Washington, is one of the hunters who's discovered the landlubber's version of the turkey boat: a mountain bike.

Like the boat, the bike affords hunters the opportunity to hunt public lands that are all but inaccessible to sportspeople on foot.

"We have a lot of timber-company land out here that's open to the public," says Miller. "Many of the companies have begun gating their roads to keep out poachers and to curtail littering problems. Vehicles and four-wheelers aren't allowed, but hunters on foot, horseback, and bicycles are."

Most hunters won't walk more than a mile or two beyond the gate. Miller might cover up to 10 miles in an hour of biking, giving him access to thousands of acres that rarely see another hunter.

Although timber-company roads are usually well maintained, Miller takes the precaution of scouting them during daylight in the preseason. "I'll sometimes take a flashlight along to see in the dark, and I always wear a helmet," he says. "My friends give me a hard time about the helmet, but on some of those steep hills I have to get off and push the bike up; going down the other side, I really get moving."

In areas where roads are closed to vehicular traffic, turkeys often use roads as strut zones and dusting areas. Miller has found that the bike allows him to move quietly through prime habitat.

"I'll ride 200 or 300 yards and call, listen for a minute, and ride down the road," he says. "One of the real beauties of the bike as opposed to a four-wheeler is that I can hear birds while I'm riding. Several times I've heard gobbles in the distance while I've been pedaling down the trail."

At the end of the hunt, Miller simply packs the turkey on his back and rides out.

The turkey boat has one great advantage over the bike: When the turkeys aren't gobbling, you can always bag hunting and go fishing. One May three of us took a 16-foot Lund out onto Iowa's Lake Rathbun on a blustery cold spring day. We probed the inlets of Rathbun all morning with loud yelps and cutts to no avail. My math teacher used to say, "If you're stuck, write the problem another way." We rewrote "turkey" like this: C-R-A-P-P-I-E.

On the local game warden's advice, we pulled the boat into the marina, where, he'd assured us, anyone could catch a crappie. Mooring the boat in one of the slips, we fished among the floating docks with no success. Then, a fisherman of about 75 walked out onto the ramp with a rod and an empty stringer. If he had been a turkey hunter, he would have been the kind who sits still for hours, emitting the occasional soft cluck. He fished deep and slow, letting the jig hang motionless about 10 feet below the surface. As he moved from slip to slip, he held his lengthening stringer furtively along his side like a quarterback bootlegging a football, but we noticed anyway and began imitating his method. We'd feel only the faintest tickle of a crappie nibbling our yellow tube jigs as a signal to set the hook. Once we found the right depth and the soft touch, we went to work gathering raw materials for a serious fish fry. The turkeys could wait until tomorrow.

Is there ever a time to leave the boat home in the driveway? As a matter of fact, yes, and the day after our crappie binge provided a perfect example. Windy days are bad enough for turkey hunters trying to hear distant gobblers on land, but in a boat the loud slap of waves against the hull makes hearing even more difficult.

"We can take the boat today or we can shoot a turkey, but we can't do both," my guide offered when we saw the trees swaying and the rain clouds gathering the next morning. He'd scouted a ridge overlooking the lake where he knew birds roosted, so there was no need to cover lots of ground, he explained. And by walking in from above the roost on dry land, we wouldn't have to worry sneaking up and around them, as we would have to if we came in from the lake shore.

He twisted my arm. I voted to leave the boat and shoot a turkey. Two toms came gobbling up the hill together 20 minutes after dawn. I set the sights on a bright head and touched off the blackpowder shotgun. The wind whipped the curtain of white smoke away from the muzzle, revealing just one turkey flying back down toward the water. The bird I shot weighed 21 pounds, not especially big for my part of the world, but an awkward, heavy load nevertheless. Before we'd walked far, I was wishing for a boat to help me haul him out.

13

Fall Hunting

OUR FOREFATHERS hunted turkeys the year round, but we are, by and large, a nation of spring turkey hunters today. Folks who've never tried a fall hunt disdain the idea of shooting hens and poults. The real excitement of turkey hunting, they sniff, lies in hearing the birds gobble.

I am here to tell you that the sight of 25 turkeys piling over a hilltop intent on kicking your tailfeathers will change your mind about fall hunting in a hurry.

So will sitting stock-still at the scatter point not knowing which way to turn as unseen turkeys whistle to relocate one another all around you. If you ever set up under 60 or 70 roosted birds on a fall morning, you'll hear more varied turkey sounds (including gobbles) in an hour than you'll hear in a whole spring season.

When you finally shoot a 10-pound hen or a bird of the year and roast it whole, you'll start to wonder why we ever bother with those big ugly gobblers in the spring at all. Not only that, the lessons you learn in the fall will make you a better hunter come spring.

SCATTERING THE FLOCK

The classic method of fall hunting is scattering a flock. What you do is, and I'm not making this up, spot a flock, sneak in close, then run into the middle of it, screaming, waving your arms, perhaps even shooting into the air. If you've done it right, turkeys flush in all directions. Then you sit down and call them back.

It's imperative, however, that you really do scatter the flock. If

Eleven states allow the use of dogs in the fall season to scatter flocks. This trained turkey dog then waits patiently inside its camouflaged bag. *Photo by Julia C. McClellan.*

they all fly off together, or, worse, run away as a flock, you're out of luck. You need the turkeys to be looking for each other and trying to regroup for this method to work. While you can bust up a flock any time of day, many hunters like to scatter birds as they're going to roost at night, returning first thing in the morning to set up and call. Others like to slip in to the roost early in the morning and break up the flock right after flydown.

Pick a tree close to the scatter point, set up and wait 5 minutes and start to *kee kee* or use the "assembly call," a long series of 15 or more hen yelps. Think "lost" and try to get some plaintive urgency into your calling. Very shortly, you'll hear birds around you whistling and looking for one another.

It's possible to scatter flocks of gobblers, too. Longbeards fre-

Ray Eye packs out a fall gobbler. *Photo courtesy of Ray Eye.*

quently spend the fall in bunches of six or seven. You can call them with the same tactics you use on the young of the year, but you'll need an extra dose of patience to do it. Scattered toms might not start looking for one another for up to an hour after the flush, and they'll take their time coming to your slow, coarse gobbler yelps.

New York and Virginia are the strongholds of fall hunting with dogs; the concept is the same as a normal fall hunt, but the dog does the legwork. A turkey dog (and yes, it is a breed) covers the woods, sniffs out turkeys, and charges into the flock. After they scatter, the dog remains at the flush site, barking so the hunters can find him and set up. From there on out, the caller takes over, just as in a dogless hunt. The dog, his work done, crawls into a camo bag and waits with the hunter in case he's needed for a retrieve. Fall hunting with dogs, alas, is legal only in a handful of states.

PECKING ORDER

Scattering the flock isn't the only way to hunt fall turkeys.

"Where I grew up in the Ozarks, you might hunt four or five days without seeing a turkey. It didn't make any sense to me to run 'em off once I finally found 'em," says Ray Eye. Rather than scattering turkeys and recalling them, Eye takes advantage of the turkey's highly developed social structure to call in whole flocks of birds.

"Turkeys are just like dogs or deer," Eye explains. "The flock has a rigid pecking order, and each bird has its own secure place in their little turkey world. If you can get close to a flock and sound like a new turkey, they'll try to call you to them. When you don't go to them, they'll come to you, running, posturing, purring, curious to see who you are and where you'll fit into their social order."

In the fall, gobblers, jakes, and hens all gather in separate flocks. Calling like a hen to fall gobblers brings no response; to upset the pecking order, you need to be a new gobbler. Same thing with jakes and hens.

Eye always begins a fall hunt at dawn, close to a roost. "Every morning when they wake up they have to fuss and bicker for an hour, sorting themselves out and getting the whole flock organized," says Eye, "They can't go on about their day until every bird is in its proper place."

If the early morning hunt doesn't produce a turkey, Eye will walk and call, just like a spring hunter trying to strike a gobbler. Eye's basic fall locating call is a long series of plaintive yelps, a generic lost call. When turkeys respond, he answers in kind—replying with hen calls to hens, jake calls to jakes—mimicking the bird's calls and upping the intensity with each exchange. To make Eye's style of hunting work, you need to get close and call aggressively.

One October afternoon I followed Eye, scuttling half-crouched across a northeast Missouri pasture, as we tried to get around a flock of birds we'd spotted heading into a wooded draw. "Sit there," he whispered, "there" being a patch of bare pasture in grass roughly the height of the manicured turf on a putting green. When Eye yelped, the flock of young birds responded with whistles. Eye countered, trading whistled insults with the unseen birds until we could hear them running up the side of the draw, feet rattling the dry leaves, making as much noise as a dozen men sprinting toward us. The flock crested the hill, led by an old hen, who skidded to a halt when she spotted us, then took off on the run. "Shoot that one," commanded Eye, so I did, after which he made fun of me for shooting the only hen in the bunch. Me, I could care less; that hen was a trophy from one of the most exciting turkey hunts I've ever been on, and she was a lot easier to carry out of the woods than a 22-pound gobbler anyway. Incidentally, the flock had scattered at my shot, and 20 minutes later Eye *kee keed* in a young bird for the other hunter who was with us that day.

If your conscience or vanity doesn't permit you to shoot a hen or bird of the year, Eye can tell you how to call up a fall longbeard.

"People kill hens in the fall because they make hen calls," he explains. "If you want to shoot a fall longbeard, you have to talk gobbler talk."

Gobbler yelps don't always sound like the long, low croaks you hear in contests or on instructional tapes. Actually, they're similar to hen yelps, but each yelp is drawn out, and at a slower cadence. Like hens, gobblers will also putt and cutt when they're excited. For gobbler calling, Eye uses a call with a clear tone and a raspy finish.

Spring hunters know gobblers will be near hens, but that's not true in the fall. "Gobblers are no different than mature whitetails," Eye points out, "They keep to themselves. You won't find fall longbeards in the same place you see hens, jakes, and poults."

Eye advises fall gobbler hunters to look for 4- to 4½-inch tracks, big droppings, and black-edged breast feathers. Find the roost and their food source, then try to get in between them on the turkey's line of travel. If you're pushy enough on the call, six or seven mature gobblers might just run to you, beards swinging, ready to fight. Make them really mad, and they'll strut and gobble as they come in, even though it's mid-October and the leaves are glowing red and gold.

FALL TACTICS FOR SPRING TURKEYS

The lessons learned in October can help you tag a gobbler in April.

Eddie Salter, another Hunters Specialties pro-staffer, likes to use the scatter on tough, henned-up gobblers in the spring.

"I go in at dusk and scatter the gobbler and his hens off the roost. I feel like we're athletes playing a sport and that tough turkey has the home field advantage. If I scatter him off his home field, I break him out of his routine, and the next morning when he wakes up he won't have those hens sitting right there with him. He'll act like a completely different bird. Most of the time when you scatter a gobbler like that, you kill him 20 minutes into the hunt the next day."

Turkey pecking-order tactics work year round as well. In fact, Eye first learned to use pecking order to his advantage on a spring morning in the Ozarks, 25 years ago.

"I was watching my brother call to a gobbler with hens out in a field. Marty was doing a fine job of calling, but the gobbler wanted to strut with his hens." Eye, meanwhile, was trying to figure out a way to shoot his brother's bird; pecking order is pretty important in some human flocks, too.

"A pair of toms appeared at the far edge of the field, and one yelped. My brother's gobbler dropped out of strut, ran to the end of the field, chased one bird off, beat the stuffing out of the other, then came back to his hens. I snuck around to that end of the field and made the same gobbler yelp. Marty's came running. He was ready to whip me. Isn't it just like a turkey to bring spurs to a gunfight?"

Whether you hunt in the fall to tune up for spring or to learn more about your favorite bird, you'll quickly discover fall hunting to be very much its own reward.

14

Western Turkeys

MERRIAM'S and Rio Grande turkeys roam the plains, prairies, mountains, and scrubland of the West that no timber-loving eastern or Osceola wild turkey could ever call home. The rap on western turkeys is they're, well, kind of stupid.

Don't go west underestimating Merriam's and Rios nor the wide open spaces in which they live. You won't tag a western gobbler if you treat him like a dumb eastern turkey. Although the calls, guns, and gear are the same, hunting western birds emphasizes different skills and a different outlook.

First, western birds aren't stupid, says avid turkey hunter M. D. Johnson, who spent several years in Washington state, one of the few places in the country that has easterns, Merriam's, and Rio Grandes.

"The differences in their behaviors are due to lower population densities of turkeys, not lower IQs" says Johnson. "An eastern turkey won't travel half a mile to a call; he doesn't have to go that far to find a hen. On the other hand, I've seen Merriam's gobblers come half a mile to a call and run the last 400 yards. They're used to traveling a long way for food and water. Covering a few hundred yards to meet a hen is no big deal to a western bird."

While it's easy to spot turkeys in the West, the open terrain works against you as often as it works to your advantage. "Merriam's are up on the ridges anyway, looking down at you," notes Johnson. "There are no contiguous hardwoods to hide in. You might have to detour three-quarters of a mile out of your way just to get to the place where the belly crawling begins."

Western turkeys inhabit some wide-open spaces. Julia McClellan admires Washington's Mt. Hood with a Merriam's gobbler over her shoulder. *Photo by Julia C. McClellan.*

MERRIAM'S HUNTING

Eastern turkeys are, essentially, homebodies. Western birds roam. Forget that fact, and you're doomed to frustration when you hunt Merriam's turkeys.

"People go into an area before the season, see lots of sign, and think it's a done deal," says Johnson. "They come back on opening day, and the turkeys are gone."

Merriam's turkeys cover several miles in a day and might roost a mile or more away from wherever they spent the previous night. Moreover, they migrate. They'll winter at lower elevations, then follow the receding snowline upward with the onset of spring. The birds don't stay right with the snow; often, they're a week or so behind it.

"Timing is critical with Merriam's turkeys," says Johnson. "I think weather variables affect gobbling activity more with Merriam's than with eastern birds. The peaks of gobbling and breeding activity don't last as long. Often the bachelor groups of gobblers will migrate first. They wait for the hens and wander around in these shark packs of gobblers. If you time your hunt right, you can yelp twice and eight gobblers might run you over."

Once the gobblers gather hens, Merriam's hunters often face the challenge of calling in turkeys by the flock. "That's one of the hardest parts," says Steve Puppe, another avid hunter of western turkeys. "There are so many eyes and ears. You might call in 20 hens and 10 gobblers. The gobblers usually hang back, so you have to sit still and wait for the hens to get around you to get a shot at a gobbler."

Puppe says he often has to call to the hens, not the toms, to bring birds into range.

"When they're flocked up, hens lead the gobblers. I'll call to the hens, yelping and cutting and being very aggressive," says Puppe, "and when the hens come, the gobblers will follow.

"The birds will typically roost in ponderosa pines and like to strut in meadows. If you're used to hunting eastern birds, you'll be surprised at how far sound carries; on a still day you can hear birds 2 or 3 miles away," concludes Puppe. Like easterns, Merriam's will fly down to strut in an opening—either a meadow or farm field—first thing. Puppe tries to set up between the roost and the bird's strut zone for the early morning hunt.

Unlike hunting in many eastern states however, which ends around noon or one o'clock, western turkey hunting lasts all day, and hunters record as much or more success in the afternoon as in the early morning.

"You'll hear them crank up between noon and 2:00 P.M. like it was the first 15 minutes of daylight," says Johnson. "Again, eastern turkeys don't gobble as much, because they don't have to; there are hens everywhere. Western turkeys may have to go half a mile between girlfriends."

RIO GRANDE HUNTING

Although Rio Grande turkeys are birds of the western flatlands, not mountains and foothills, they're similar to Merriam's in many ways.

Kevin Howard doubled on these two Rio Grande gobblers in Texas. *Photo by Julia C. McClellan.*

Like Merriam's turkeys, Rios wander all over the open country they inhabit. Brad Valdois of Neosho, Missouri, hunts extensively in nearby Kansas, a state blessed with both easterns and Rios.

"You hunt easterns primarily with your ears," he says. "Rio hunting is a visual game. You can spot flocks, figure out where they're headed, and get around them to set up and call." Good binoculars are a must for Rio hunting; you use them to spot distant birds, to evaluate gobblers, and, frankly, to eliminate turkey-shaped stumps and bushes from your consideration. Once you've spotted a gobbler, or a flock, you have to use folds in the terrain to try to close the distance as best you can. Often, you'll have to set up a few hundred yards away.

"You can see a bird and not be able to get at him," says Valdois of the frustrations and rewards of Rio hunting. "At the same time, you wind up calling in birds you thought were way too far away to call, but you have no choice." Rios also depend on their keen eyesight. Sometimes a glimpse of a decoy will bring a gobbler running across a wheatfield, according to Valdois.

While Rios may be attuned to visual cues, calling—often loud, aggressive calling—remains very important.

Valdois always carries a box call when he hunts Rios. "You might be calling to a turkey 600 yards away in a high wind," he points out. "You need the volume of a box call so the turkeys can hear you."

At times, you'll have to try to call in an entire flock of Rios to get a gobbler in range. "You might be dealing with two gobblers and 15 hens in a flock," says Valdois. "Nine times out of 10 you'll call aggressively to the hens to get the flock to come your way."

As with Merriam's turkeys, scouting is crucial to successful Rio Grande hunting. "Eastern turkeys pick two or three ridges and that's it," says Valdois. "You may not hear them every morning, but you know they're there. Rios might move 5 or 6 miles in a day."

The closer to your hunt time you can scout, the better. In Kansas, for instance, Valdois has observed that the height of the wheat crop affects bird movement. "They love wheatfields until the plants reach a foot high, then they don't like them any more," explains Valdois. "I think they don't feel safe, plus [the wheat] holds lots of moisture and gets their feathers wet."

Valdois hunts both eastern and Rio Grande turkeys avidly each spring. Forced to choose one subspecies, he'd pick Rios, and not because they're supposedly easier to tag.

"It's visual hunting," he says. "Face it, when you see an eastern bird in full strut, he's probably in gun range. You might spend 2 or 3 hours in a field with a Rio where you're not in a good position to harvest him, but you can watch him. You have more opportunities to watch the mating ritual with Rios because it all happens out in the open."

Index

Howard, Kevin, 108 photo

Impoundments, 91, 95
Islands, 95

Jakes
   decoy, 81 photo, 82, 83
   description, 8
Johnson, M.D., 105, 106–107

Kansas, 109
Kee kee (call), 24, 100
Knight, Tony, 63
Knives, 41

Latex, use in calls, 15, 20
Legality
   of afternoon hunting, 61, 82
   of dog use, 100 photo, 102
   of pellet size, 27
   of rifles, 34, 86
Locating, of turkeys, 47
Locator calls, 22–23
Longbeards, 101–102, 103. *See also*
   Gobblers
Louis (turkey), 78

Maps, 47, 48, 94–95
McClellan, Julia, 87, 106 photo
McPherren, Randy, 94 photo
Meleagris gallopavo
   intermedia, 5
   merriami, 5–6, 46, 105–107
   Osceola, 6–7
   silvestris, 5, 105, 107–109
Merriam, C. Hart, 5
Merriam's turkeys, 5–6, 24, 105–107
Midday hunting, 61–66, 68, 93
Migration, of turkeys, 46, 106
Miller, John, 96
Mistaken-for-game accidents, 87–88
Morning hunting. *See* Dawn hunting;
   Midday hunting
Morrett, Matt, 15–23, 80 photo
Morton, Thomas, 10
Mountain bikes, for hunting, 96

Mouth calls. *See* Diaphragm calls;
   Tube calls
Multitools, 41
Muzzleloaders, 35–37

National Wild Turkey Federation
   (NWTF), 12, 85, 88–90
Neck shots, 34
Nesting, 8, 47
New York State, use of dogs in,
   101
Noise, 63. *See also* Silence
Notebooks, 47

Old Mossy (turkey), 77–78
Orange clothing, 62, 86
Osceola turkey, 6–7
Overshooting, 10

Pants, 42, 90
Parrot, Walter, 67–71
Patterning, of
   turkeys, 48–49, 48–50
Peep sights, 28
Pellets
   counts, 30–31
   size, 27
Pennsylvania
   game farm turkeys in, 11–12
   orange clothing in, 86
Petty, Ron, 76
Pilgrims, 10
Pittman-Robertson excise tax, 11
Pollick, Steve, 60 photo
Ponchos, 41
Poults, 8, 46
Powders, smokeless, 37
Predators, 8
Premature closure, 87–88
Primaries, 48
Primos, Will, 75–78
Pruning shears, 41, 69
Puppe, Steve, 46 photo, 87
Purrs, 24, 103
Pushbutton calls, 20
Putts, 24–25, 103